NORTH AMERICA

A WORLD IN ONE CONTINENT

by Huw Cordey

Running Press
PHILADELPHIA · LONDON

Published by Running Press,
A Member of the Perseus Books Group

Books published by Running Press are available at special discounts for bulk purchases in the United States by corporations, institutions, and other organizations. For more information, please contact the Special Markets Department at the Perseus Books Group, 2300 Chestnut Street, Suite 200, Philadelphia, PA 19103, or call (800) 810-4145, ext. 5000, or e-mail special.markets@perseusbooks.com.

ISBN 978-0-7624-4842-5
Library of Congress Control Number: 2012953087

E-book ISBN 978-0-7624-4843-2

9   8   7   6   5   4   3   2   1
Digit on the right indicates the number of this printing

Cover and interior design by Melissa Gerber
Edited by Geoffrey Stone
Typography: Adobe Garamond, Gotham, Avenir LT Std, and Goudy Oldstyle

Running Press Book Publishers
2300 Chestnut Street
Philadelphia, PA 19103-4371

Visit us on the web!
www.runningpress.com

CONTENTS

FOREWORD

North America is a land of rich biological diversity. In my work as head of The Nature Conservancy, I've been lucky enough to see some of our continent's extraordinary landscapes firsthand, from golden plains to frosted peaks, from the tangles of coral reefs to those of the jungle, from open desert expanses to mist-shrouded forests, and from peaceful ponds to rushing rivers.

From Discovery Channel and Silverback Films, comes a breathtaking story: *North America*. In this companion book to the series, Series Producer, Huw Cordey seamlessly integrates animal, wilderness and human stories. The 347 images that follow remind us of the long and colorful history of a continent so many call their home, and the fundamental imperative we all have to protect it.

For me, that imperative has never been clearer. Despite all the good work of conservationists over the years, the challenges to nature are growing more serious. Yet there is hope, especially if we can convince people that nature is not a special interest. All of our lives and livelihoods are intertwined with the survival of nature. More than ever, it is crucial that we develop innovative solutions to continue to meet the needs of a growing population without destroying the natural systems that provide us with clean air to breathe, water to drink, and healthy soils to grow our food.

Books like this and the series it accompanies are one of the ways we hope to instill in people a greater appreciation of nature. To that end, I hope the stunning photos in the pages that follow will inspire you to want to protect the spectacular wild places on our continent.

The images are extraordinary. During the production of "North America," four dozen men and women spent three years traveling from the Arctic Circle to the Panama Canal. Along the way, they encountered North America's remarkable wildlife firsthand and recorded these encounters in spectacular detail and brilliance. In their journeys, the crew assembled a picture of North America's diverse terrains and abounding flora and fauna. In these fleeting moments, they also captured the fragility of its natural wonders.

North America reminds readers of the importance of our natural heritage. For example, the beautiful cypress-draped wetlands of the Florida Everglades, home to the gentle manatee and the fearsome crocodile, also provide the main source of drinking water for millions of South Floridians. The coral reefs of Central America, where underwater cameraman Didier Noirot was the first to ever film a unique partnership between a bass and a moray eel, provide the foundation for local fisheries, tourism, and recreation economies. The rainforests of Panama, where the crew recorded the spectacular mating dance of the red-tipped manakin, supply water for the operation of the Panama Canal, soaking up water in the rainy season and slowly releasing it during drier months.

Further north the millions of horseshoe crabs that come ashore each spring in Delaware Bay contain a substance used to test the purity of medicines. And the Great Bear Rainforest of British Columbia, where the team spent ten weeks seeking the perfect shot of coastal wolves feasting on salmon, sustains the livelihoods and culture of First Nations people.

While we celebrate these places' intrinsic beauty, nature's important social and economic values—from improved water quality to increased recreational opportunities and tourism revenues—will help us move conservation from the sidelines to the mainstream. *North America* reminds us that we are all connected by our environment, and that it is our responsibility to protect the lands and waters on which all life depends.

—Mark R. Tercek, President and CEO,
The Nature Conservancy

INTRODUCTION

North America is the most extraordinary continent on earth. Stretching from the tropics of Panama to the icy wastelands of northern Canada and the Arctic, it has the greatest range of landscapes, the greatest extremes of seasons, and the most exciting variety of wildlife on the planet. It is a world in one continent, with its magnificent mountain ranges, great deserts, vast plains, breathtaking canyons, and lush forests.

Here you can experience the most extreme temperature changes in the world, and the most terrifying and brutal weather: tornadoes, hurricanes, great storms, sudden snowfall, and scorching heat. And the breathtaking natural diversity and abundance of riches that these conditions create is home to many of nature's greatest marvels, including the world's tallest, biggest, and oldest trees; a canyon that is one of the seven natural wonders of the world; the world's oldest

mountain range; and the world's largest freshwater lake.

It is a land of surprises. Who would have thought that mankind's greatest allies—the dog, the horse, and the camel—all originated in North America? Or that it is the only continent to have every kind of climate? Or that it is home to the world's tallest mountain? Measured from base to tip, Alaska's Mount McKinley/Denali is taller than Mount Everest.

With 150,000 miles of coastline, North America also has the longest and most abundant shores of any continent on earth. And its two coasts, East and West, could not be more different from one another. On the East are the warm, shallow seas of the Atlantic that produce rich corals and the world's greatest tidal ranges, and nurture a huge diversity of sea life. On the West, the vast swells of the Pacific Ocean hit the steep cliffs of the great mountain ranges that rise, harsh and jagged, from the deep.

The North American continent stretches for over 9.5 million square miles, and is home to twenty-four countries and almost 528 million people, who share it with hundreds of thousands of species of mammals, birds, insects, and plants—many of them extraordinary, unforgettable, and unique.

The Pacific Coast sees some of the largest waves on the continent. The deep waters and thousands of miles of clear ocean can cause the waves to rise as high as 33 feet (10 m).

The film crew drives though hurricane Irene as it hits North Carolina.

Bogged down in the Costa Rica rainforest.

CREATING THE NORTH AMERICA PROGRAMS

Our team spent over three years filming the natural wonders of this great continent to make a landmark series of programs. It was an enormous challenge deciding where to go, what to include, and how to capture the dramatic and unpredictable weather events and the often extraordinary behaviors of creatures in their natural habitat, from the courtship dance of the tiny jumping spider, to the death-defying fishing techniques of a small band of bottlenose dolphins, to the struggle for survival of thousands of baby turtles on the tropical beaches of the South.

We wanted to discover the heart of North America—the places, natural events, and animal and plant life that gives this continent its unique character, and to show its weather shifts, landscapes, and wildlife through a fresh lens. And we wanted to capture imaginations with a series that would include the most remote corners of the continent and its animals, as they had never been filmed before. To make the kind of programs we wanted would mean getting camera teams and equipment to out-of-the-way places, like Labrador, the Aleutian Islands, and the depths of the Panamanian jungle, and then setting up camp for several weeks—and this would require plenty of time, a generous budget, and a great deal of planning.

The team included some of the most knowledgeable and experienced natural history filmmakers and cameramen in the world—people with a passion for nature and with determination, ingenuity, skill, and above all, endless patience. We did a huge amount of research and we also consulted some brilliant scientists and wildlife experts whose guidance, advice, and expertise helped to ensure that we were, whenever possible, in the right places at the right times.

Many of the animals in North America show the same brave and hardy spirit that characterized the early pioneers. To survive you must be tough and adaptable, and in the deserts and the snows, in the seas and the lakes, and even on the plains, there is still a great struggle for survival every single day, for creatures both large and small. More than anything else, it is this epic struggle in North America's extreme and harsh environments that we set out to capture, through the behavior of animals like the pronghorn, which migrate for

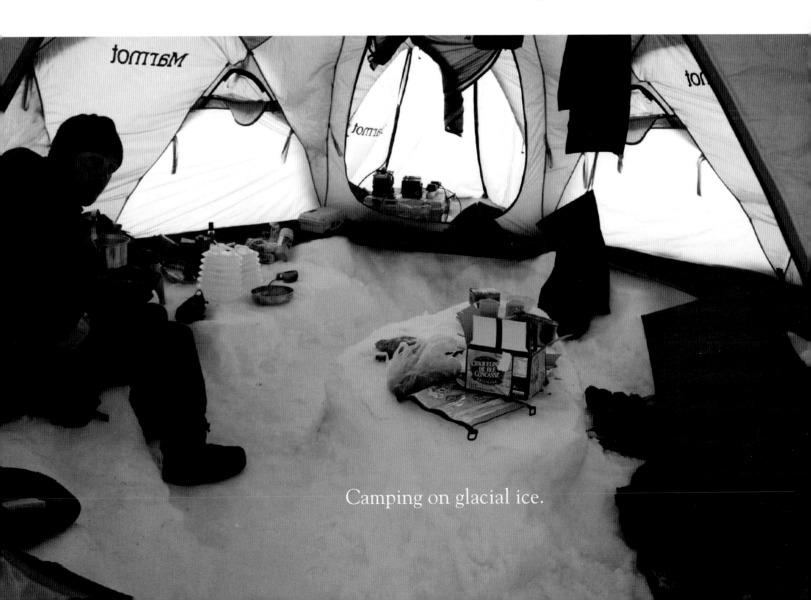

Camping on glacial ice.

Filming mountain goats in the Rockies.

extraordinary distances to find food; the spadefoot toad, which lives underground most of its life to avoid the heat of the desert; and the all-American coyote, so tough and adaptable that it can survive in temperatures as low as -50°F (-46°C) in the bitter chill of Yellowstone, or as high as 120°F (49°C) in the blistering heat of Death Valley.

Of course, animals don't always do what you expect them to do, and neither does the weather, so sometimes you have to tear your plans up and start again. You can wait weeks for a special moment that doesn't come, or for the arrival of an animal that doesn't show up. But it can work the other way too—extraordinary things can happen that make all the planning, watching, and waiting worthwhile; a mother prairie dog confronting a rattlesnake to protect her young, a bobcat playing catch with a gopher, or the world's smallest rabbit outwitting a weasel.

In all, we spent 2,830 days in the field, with 51 cameramen and women on 250 shoots, in 10 countries, 29 US states, and 8 Canadian provinces, filming hundreds of animals in over 100 different locations, with several shoots in progress at any one time. At the end of it all, we had to reduce many hundreds of hours of filming to six hours of blue-chip natural history programming. It wasn't easy, but the result is a series we are proud of.

In the following pages, we have attempted to recapture the programs and the stories behind them in words and photographs, and to include some of the details, as well as the amazing tales, that didn't make our final edit.

The episodes focus on particular types of terrain—the plains, mountains, forests, deserts, rivers, and oceans and their weather and wildlife. But for the opening film, we wanted to give a flavor of the whole North American continent, to capture the variety of the land, the unpredictable power of its weather, and the richness and beauty of the animal life. So we begin with the two ends of the continent, three thousand miles apart; the Far North and the Deep South, the icy tundra of Labrador in northeastern Canada, and the tropical forests and beaches of Costa Rica, to illustrate just how magical and extraordinary the places and creatures were that we discovered on our incredible journey.

Prairie fires quickly engulf the plains.

CHAPTER ONE

BORN TO BE WILD

To begin to know North America, with its rich mix of dramatic and breathtaking beauty, unpredictable cruelty, and unique wildlife, you need to take a brief look back at its history to understand how the continent came into being and the forces of time and nature that shaped it. North America became what it is through millions of years of upheaval and change, and through its physical connections to two other continents: South America and Asia. These land bridges meant that mammals, birds, reptiles, insects, and plants could cross back and forth between continents, and many did just that, creating a blend of flora and fauna that became distinctively and unmistakably North American in character.

As the land gradually took shape, throwing up its mountain ranges, flattening its plains, drying out its deserts, and seeding its forests, the weather patterns that are more distinct and changeable than any in the world, gradually evolved.

THE BIRTH OF THE NORTH AMERICAN CONTINENT

Many millions of years ago, North America was two land-masses with a sea known as the Bearpaw Sea between them. The eastern land block was geologically constant. Its only mountain range, the Appalachians, began to form over 450 million years ago—making them the oldest mountain range on the planet—and became a strong and stable backbone, while its eastern coast gradually eroded and subsided into the sea, creating a gentle shelf.

The western landmass, by contrast, was geologically restless. It had been joined to Asia by the Bering land bridge and its fauna and flora were largely shared with Asia. Its mountain range was the Sierra Nevada, a jagged range of recently extinct volcanoes. The Rocky Mountains did not yet exist, and the coastline plummeted dramatically into the Pacific. Oregon, Washington, and parts of California were still islands out at sea.

These two landmasses were brought together after a huge asteroid struck earth sixty-five million years ago. Together they formed what would become North America. Across the center where the Bearpaw Sea had been, lay vast stretches of forest that would eventually erode into the Great Plains.

North America was separate from South America and it was a mere 2.8 million years ago that the land connection

between them appeared. The impact of this narrow Panamanian land bridge was enormous. For the first time, animals were able to travel between these two continents and they did, in huge numbers. This exchange of species that had developed independently for tens of millions of years was described by famous paleontologist George Gaylord Simpson as "one of the most extraordinary events in the whole history of life."

While the land bridge joined the continents, it separated the two seas on either side of it, and though it was, and still is, only thirty miles wide, it meant that species now belonged to one sea or the other, and could no longer travel between them.

The animals that traveled into North America from South America joined those that had originated in North America and those that had been arriving, over millions of years, through the land connections to Europe, via Greenland—a connection that was severed forty-five million years ago—and to Asia, via the Bering land bridge, which did not disappear under the sea until around 13,500 years ago. The result was an extraordinarily rich and varied array of wildlife, which has continuously evolved to the present day. No other continent has living species from such different origins. Today the mammals of North America are largely Eurasian, the migratory land birds are largely South American, and its reptiles and amphibians are unique.

The last ice age began around thirty-five thousand years ago and reached its peak eighteen thousand years ago. While global temperatures dropped by an average of four to five degrees, the changes were amplified in North America where the drop was eight to ten degrees, and the continent was covered with more ice than Antarctica. The ice was so heavy that, following the melting of the ice twelve thousand years ago, the continent is still rising. These massive ice caps

Central America

Although many people assume Central America is a separate continent, it is actually the southernmost part of the North American continent. There are seven countries in Central America: Belize, El Salvador, Guatemala, Honduras, Costa Rica, Nicaragua, and Panama. Nicaragua is the largest and Belize the smallest. Spanish is the official language in all the countries apart from Belize, where English is spoken.

The Caribbean islands, separating the Gulf of Mexico and the Caribbean Sea from the Atlantic, are also considered to be a part of North America. There are more than seven thousand islands, islets, reefs, and cays. The largest is Cuba and the others include the Bahamas, Jamaica, Antigua, the Cayman Islands, Puerto Rico, Saint Lucia, and Trinidad and Tobago.

Alaska was purchased from the Russians in 1867 for $7.2 million ($120 million in today's dollars)—that is, about two cents an acre. It became the forty-ninth state on January 3, 1959, seven months before Hawaii became the fiftieth state.

Death Valley in California is one of the hottest and most hostile places in the world.

were hugely significant to the future of North America; they ploughed up the land, generating huge quantities of fresh, new soil and leaving it a richly fertile continent.

The Americas were the last continents to be occupied by humans, who arrived via the Bering land connection and then traveled down through North America to South America. Although some scientists believe there was an earlier human presence, the vast majority believe only thirteen thousand years have passed since the first people arrived—forty thousand years after humans reached Australasia—Australia, New Zealand, New Guinea, and adjacent islands. These earliest inhabitants, known as the Clovis people (named after a town in eastern New Mexico near which artifacts were found), were hunters. They used spearheads known as Clovis points, which have been found throughout North America. Within three hundred years of their arrival, three quarters of all large animals over one hundred pounds (45 kg) including mammoths, giant sloths, camels, and giant bison had

disappeared, and although it is possible that climate change played a part in this, the most likely theory is that the Clovis people and their deadly spearheads were responsible.

The North American horses, the camel, the saber tooth, the mammoth, giant beavers and sloths, the short-faced bear, and a number of other large species were all completely wiped out. These creatures had evolved without any human predators, so when humans arrived, the animals were not afraid of them and were easy prey. This is in contrast to Africa, where humans and large animals, such as elephants, evolved together and the animals' wariness toward humans has, in part, enabled them to survive.

Horses would later return to North America with the Spanish colonists and bison, grizzly bears, elk, and moose all arrived around the time of the Clovis people via Eurasia, while the sloth and the opossum arrived via the bridge to South America.

With temperatures falling to fifty below, the pines of northern Canada become stunted but still form the largest forests of the continent.

North America is the third largest continent in the world, after Asia and Africa. It is bigger than South America, Antarctica, Europe, and Australia.

THE NORTH AMERICAN CLIMATE

With its head in the Arctic and its feet just above the equator, North America includes a huge climatic range. With no mountain ranges running east to west across the continent to provide a climatic barrier, the dry, icy winds of the north are funneled by the north-south mountain ranges to meet the moist, warm winds coming up from the south. The result is extraordinary extremes of weather and short-term temperature shifts that hit many parts of the continent. For instance, in Spearfish, South Dakota, the temperature once went from -2°F to 38°F (-19°C to 3°C) in just two minutes—the world's fastest recorded change in temperature! This clashing of north and south winds over the plains also creates huge storms, many of which spawn tornadoes.

The weather can change dramatically fast and can be dangerously unpredictable, and sometimes deadly. Huge tropical downpours, lightning storms, snowfall and avalanches, harsh winters, brief springs, and sizzling summers are all regular occurrences. The fauna of North America—its mammals, birds, amphibians, and insects—have had to cope with these changes and those that have been able to adapt,

to withstand extreme temperatures, to vary their diet, or survive long periods of famine, have flourished. The result is a rich variety of truly fascinating creatures that capture the imagination, from the tiny, inch-long hummingbird that can shut its body down at night to outwit the desert chill, to the ungainly but gentle manatee, which can only survive by taking advantage of the warmth of the Florida springs, to the nimble swift fox that gets through the bitter winter chill because it can hear—and catch—a mouse through 3 feet (1 m) of snow.

We wanted to record North America's dramatic and sudden climate variations, but this proved difficult during our first year of filming, which was an El Niño year. El Niño is a weather event that occurs every three to seven years, during which there are prolonged temperature anomalies in the surface of the Pacific that can wreak havoc with normal weather patterns. Weather experts were able to predict that it was coming, but not how strong it would be, or its impact. So we had to plan our filming knowing that the weather might change our plans and that the animals might not respond in their usual ways. Fortunately we had a second year of filming and were able to revisit places where El Niño had disrupted both the weather and the wildlife.

Labrador, about twice the size of the US state of Colorado, is on the northeastern tip of the Canadian mainland and is far enough north to attract polar bears.

THE FROZEN NORTH: CARIBOU, BLACK BEARS, AND WOLVES

In the wild and inhospitable far northeast of Canada, just outside the Arctic Circle, the temperatures barely rise above freezing, and there is deep snow on the ground for most of the year. Even in the short three months of summer, there is a distinct chill in the air.

This beautiful but desolate part of the world is largely uninhabited, and is one of the most remote and unknown corners of North America: the province of Newfoundland and Labrador. Newfoundland is an island surrounded by the North Atlantic, and Labrador is part of the mainland. And though Labrador is larger than the state of Colorado, its population of mostly native Inuit people is only around twenty thousand. There are few roads and most of the province is a vast wilderness that is impossible to get around, except by dogsled or helicopter and, on the coastal areas, by boat.

We went by helicopter from the small town of Nain to the banks of a fjord three hours north, where we planned to set up a base camp. Ten months earlier, we'd had to ship forty-two drums of spare fuel by boat up to the banks of the fjord so that we could take the helicopter up there, because there was nowhere we could refuel. So when we arrived, we were extremely relieved to see the drums of fuel still sitting on the banks of the fjord.

There is very little wildlife on the icy tundra, but we knew that with the right conditions, patience, and a little luck, we would be able to film extraordinary sights that would make our journey more than worthwhile. And there were three animals in particular that we wanted to film; caribou and the wolves and black bears that prey on them.

Caribou, the largest members of the reindeer family, migrate to this area in the summers. The route they take from the sheltered southern forests where they winter to the tundra of Labrador is over 600 miles (965 km) and it's not uncommon for herds to travel 1,864 miles (3,000 km) every year.

In the recent past, only fifteen or twenty years ago, herds of hundreds of thousands of caribou have been known to travel together, creating a spectacular sight. Their long journey, crossing rivers, forests, and plains is one of the world's greatest large animal migrations. But in recent years the herds have decreased dramatically and experts have not yet been able to fully explain why.

The caribou travel to Labrador's remote terrain because the relative lack of predators makes it a safe place to have their young, and the brief Arctic summer means there is an abundance of tundra grasses and plants to eat.

The pregnant females arrive first, followed a few weeks later by the males and the yearlings. They roam over the tundra all day long, constantly on the move, and stopping only to graze. The calves are able to stand within a couple of hours of birth and can move on with the herd by the next day.

Finding the caribou in the vastness of northern Labrador was far from easy, especially now that the herds are smaller. We flew hundreds of miles, searching the terrain below for them. A small number of caribou have radio collars so that scientists can track their movements, and we would be alerted if a

Our Night Visitor

Our most terrifying experience in Labrador came when we set up camp for the night in a log-hunting cabin on the edge of a fjord. Before we settled into our bunks for the night, our helicopter pilot, Jeff, fixed the broken lock on the cabin door, and closed the wooden window shutters on the outside of the glass. Little did we know how thankful we would be for his actions. We woke in the night to hear what we were pretty sure was a bear sniffing around. Believing it was a relatively harmless black bear, we didn't worry—until there was an almighty thump on the door. We couldn't see what was happening, but it seemed the bear must be on its hind legs, battering the door with its front paws.

It tried several more times while we could only wait, hoping the lock would hold out, before it eventually gave up. The next morning we stepped cautiously outside to find that our helicopter, parked nearby, had been the bear's next port of call. It had managed to get inside, pop out the side windows, rip up the pilot's seat, and walk all over our expensive state-of-the-art camera unit.

Down toward the fjord, we found the enormous telltale pug marks of a bear. But this was no black bear; it was the most dangerous predator on Earth, the only creature that has been known to hunt human beings—a polar bear. It had been twenty-five years since a polar bear was seen that far south of the Arctic in Labrador, but when we returned to the same spot a year later to film again, there was a polar bear waiting for us. Smelling a source of food—us—we were pretty sure the same bear had returned to try its luck again.

Silver Springs, Florida, is home of one of the largest artesian springs in the world. The aquifer produces nearly 550 million gallons of crystal-clear water a day and sustains an underwater world teeming with fish, turtles, crustaceans and fossils more than 10,000 years old.

handful of these tracking devices were in one spot, indicating the possible presence of a herd. It took three to four weeks looking every day, sometimes finding herds, sometimes not, filming as often as possible to get the best footage.

Recent technological advances have made it possible to film animals from a helicopter without disturbing or frightening them. A helicopter can't fly too close to animals without panicking them, and until recently we could only get long-distance shots from the air. But with the development of gyro-stabilized cameras, we can now film detailed images from a distance.

Black bears are normally forest animals. Those that live on the open plains of Labrador are also known as barren ground bears and are larger than other black bears, and to survive the harsh sub-Arctic winters, they've had to adapt. The black bear's normal diet is roots and vegetation, but these bigger

bears need extra protein in the form of meat, which usually means caribou. They can't outrun the caribou, so they must rely on the element of surprise when hunting, lurking behind rocks and waiting for their opportunity to pounce.

We soon discovered that while the bears might have been hard to spot from the air, on the ground, they came to us. We spent six weeks at our base camp, and despite the electric fence surrounding it, we were charged by black bears several times. These bears had probably never encountered humans before and were curious, so although we would never harm any animal, we did, at times like this, fire shots into the air to scare them off. In one instance, a bear actually came over the fence and ran between our tents. After that event, visiting the latrine at night became a nerve-racking event involving a shovel and a shotgun.

While some bears were eager to discover more about us,

the wolves were far more elusive. Eventually we spotted an adult pair and were able to follow them back to their den, where there were nine hungry pups waiting to be fed. We set up a camp nearby, and for several days we watched these beautiful pups snoozing, romping, and play-fighting with one another while their parents hunted.

Unlike the bears, wolves have the stamina to track the caribou for many miles. In this area, wolves generally hunt in pairs rather than packs, so we followed our pair of wolves as they traveled over thirty miles before they found a herd. The female trapped a tiny calf against a rock, while the male set his sights on a bigger one. For several minutes, we watched as the calf was isolated from its mother and tried frantically to escape, but as the rest of the caribou scattered, the tenacious wolf brought down his quarry.

Nature is all about survival. To feed their pups, the adult wolves kill caribou calves, but the wolves' own young are also at risk. To a hungry bear, a wolf cub would make a tasty meal, and when a black bear strayed too close to the den, the wolves weren't about to let it get close to their young and they attacked. Although these fights between wolves and bears have rarely been witnessed, during the time we camped close to the wolf den, we recorded five separate occasions when black bears approached and wolves fought them off.

Remarkable moments like these, the vastness and isolation of the tundra, and our encounters with wolves, black bears, and even a polar bear (see sidebar "Our Night Visitor" on page 38) made our trips to Labrador extraordinary and memorable experiences that produced some of the rarest sights and the most exciting film footage of the series.

Coral reefs, or rainforests of the sea, are colonies of tiny living animals that form some of the most diverse ecosystems in the world.

THE TROPICAL SOUTH: OLIVE RIDLEY TURTLES AND JAGUARS

At the other end of the continent are the tropical forests and golden beaches of Costa Rica. The beaches are wide, sandy, and lined by warm blue seas. But there's something very special about one of these beaches—Nancite, in the Santa Rosa National Park. This is where the olive ridley turtles gather by the thousands to lay their eggs. Why they prefer this particular beach is a mystery since another beach nearby is wider, cleaner, and more beautiful. But the turtles return faithfully, time and time again, to the same beach where they were born.

Turtles will nest individually, but at certain times during the nesting season, they will gather offshore. As more and more heads bob in the water, it becomes clear that an *arribada* is imminent. This means "great arrival" in Spanish, and it is the mass, synchronized nesting of thousands of turtles.

At a given moment, on some unseen cue that we don't yet recognize or understand, they swim to the shore and wave after wave of three-feet-long female turtles walk the fifty yards up the beach, dig their holes, lay their eggs, and walk back to the sea. There are so many of them that the newest arrivals inevitably dig up many of the eggs laid by those who have gone before them.

Although the arribada happens at night, it continues into the dawn. We filmed it using low light and infrared cameras, and it's an astonishing sight to witness; if you stand on the beach, the turtles will simply march past you, intent on only one thing—getting their eggs into the sand. It is awe-inspiring to think that this same scene has been happening for millions of years.

Turtles are quite solitary creatures for most of the time, living far out in the waters of the vast Pacific, and although experts are still not sure why the arribada occurs, it is thought to be an opportunity firstly for males and females to get together to mate, and secondly to give the eggs the

The olive ridley is considered the most abundant sea turtle in the world, with an estimated 800,000 nesting females annually.

best chance of survival, swamping potential predators through numbers.

The arribada can—but doesn't always—happen twice a month during the wet season, when the weather is cooler and the eggs are less likely to become overheated in the sand. Over a few days, there can be as many as thirty thousand turtles nesting on this one relatively small stretch of beach. And then, as suddenly as it began, it is over; the beach is quiet and the only evidence that remains is churned up sand scattered with the eggs.

In the aftermath, all kinds of predators arrive to eat the eggs. Raccoons and coyotes dig up buried eggs, while crabs, iguanas, and hawks scoop up the exposed ones.

The next act of this great drama commences when wave after wave of tiny newly hatched turtles begin the perilously long fifty-yard walk back down to the sea. The adult turtles can weigh up to one hundred pounds (45 kg), but the new hatchlings weigh only around an ounce (28 g).

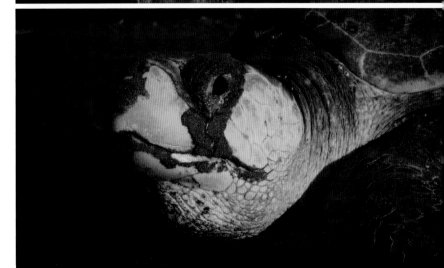

The turtles hatch at night when the sand is cooler, but as the dawn breaks and a million baby turtles are still crawling slowly down the beach, black vultures, turkey vultures, and frigate birds swoop down to scoop them up.

Those that aren't taken by the birds risk being burned alive if they don't make it to the water before the sun heats the sand. And even those that do make it into the waves are not out of danger; waiting for them are crocodiles, sharks, and other predatory fish. For a baby turtle to make it past all these dangers and survive to adulthood is a little like winning the lottery.

A similar turtle-nesting event takes place a little further south, on the Pacific side of the Isthmus of Panama—and curiously, it also happens on the opposite side of the Isthmus, on the Atlantic shore. How is it that the same species of turtle appears on both sides of this thirty-mile divide, when turtles can barely haul themselves sixty feet up the beach? The answer lies more than three million years back. Before the land bridge was established, the turtles, whose ancestors first took to the water sixty million years ago, were able to swim back and forth between the two oceans. Today they are one of the few marine creatures to be found in both oceans.

Adult turtles, with their thick, hard shells, do not have many predators, but jaguars, among the most elusive and secretive of the big cats, do enjoy feasting on turtle meat. The turtle is a relatively easy target for a jaguar, whose powerful jaws can crack the thick shell as if it were a nut, and is an ideal food source during the turtles' nesting season. For the jaguar, it is a nice change from their usual diet of, among other things, peccaries (wild pigs), tapirs, and monkeys.

On Nancite, the forest backs onto the beach, and when the turtles arrive at night, jaguar stalk the beach before pouncing and dragging their prey into the cover of the trees. The turtles put up a fight, flapping valiantly, but it is a rare turtle, once caught, that will escape a jaguar.

Once the kill is made, the jaguar will return to it over a period of days. But finding these kills is difficult, and for several weeks we had no luck until, toward the end of our shoot we found a freshly dead turtle in the forest, covered in jaguar prints. We set up night-camera traps and twice recorded an adult jaguar returning to a kill. Then on December 25, we hit gold. The cameras had recorded the rare and remarkable sight of a mother jaguar and her two cubs feasting on a fresh turtle kill. It was the best Christmas present we could have had.

The most vulnerable time for a
hatchling turtle is the dash from the
beach to the sea. Not all make it. Here
a frigate bird snatches one off the sand.

The United States

Of the 528 million people living in North America, over 312 million—well over half—live in the United States of America. The United States is the second largest North American country, after Canada, but is far more heavily populated—Canada has only thirty-four million people, as much of it is the sparsely inhabited frozen north.

The United States covers 3.8 million square miles (9.8 million sq km), which is over a third of the entire North American area. It is the third largest country in the world, after Russia and Canada, and has the third largest population, after China and India, but is the world's largest economy. The United States is one of the most ethnically diverse and multicultural nations on Earth.

The first inhabitants of the United States were the Native Americans, who descended from forebears who migrated from Asia. The United States began as thirteen British colonies along the Atlantic coast, but defeated the British in the American Revolutionary War, and the United States of America became a nation on July 4, 1776, when the Declaration of Independence proclaimed its right to self-determination.

CHAPTER TWO

NO PLACE TO HIDE

Great Plains

North America's Great Plains are about five hundred miles (805 km) east to west and two thousand miles (3,219 km) north to south. They make up approximately one million square miles (2,589,988 square kilometres) or about one-fourth of the United States, which covers parts of ten states (Montana, North Dakota, South Dakota, Wyoming, Nebraska, Kansas, Colorado, Oklahoma, Texas, and New Mexico) and the three Canadian provinces (Manitoba, Saskatchewan, and Alberta).

THE UNFORGIVING FRONTIER

The Great Plains have come to symbolize the Wild West. They stretch for an astonishing one million square miles (2.59 million sq km) of open lands and blue skies.

Situated halfway between the tropics and the polar circles, the plains are among the temperate regions of the earth. They stretch across the heart of the continent from Texas in the south to northern Canada, and from the Rocky Mountains in the west to the great Mississippi River in the east, making up more than a quarter of the United States. In Canada, they lay across the provinces of Alberta, Saskatchewan, and Manitoba, while in the United States, they extend into ten states, including Wyoming, Kansas, Colorado, Nebraska, and North and South Dakota.

The plains are dry—often tinder dry. Nestled right in the middle of the continental landmass of North America and to the west of the great mountain ranges, the Rockies, the Cascades, and the Sierras block moisture from the ocean, leaving the plains starved of rain.

If there is plenty of moisture, temperatures are moderate, but without it, the plains are subject to extreme temperature swings, in some areas from as low as -40°F (-40°C) in the winter to a high of 104°F (40°C) in the summer.

Trees do not do well in these parched conditions and give way to grasslands. Grass is the ultimate survivor; versatile and tough and able to withstand all kinds of conditions. And though grass may seem dull in comparison to forests and jungles, there is a huge variety of grasses on the plains; around 140 different species, from the big bluestem that can grow up to ten feet (3 m) tall, to the stubby buffalo grass and the tiny blue grama which grows close to the ground, with its elegant curving seed heads shaped like eyelashes.

Grass has the ability to conserve water, and can survive long periods of fierce heat and drought as well as the great fires that often sweep through the plains in summer. When the land is tinder-dry, a single spark can start a fire that is swept for miles by gusting winds, and can last for days.

Prairie fires are nature's way of starting over. Nutrients that are locked up in decaying plants are released into the soil within seconds.

Today huge areas of the plains have been cultivated and turned into agricultural lands. But the great prairies of old are still there, even if they are dotted now with towns, cities, and farms. And these great tracts of land are full of animals, even if they aren't always easy to see. Shelter is scarce and the wildlife of the plains must survive predators as well as the scorching summers and freezing winters, so many of the inhabitants live not on the land but under it. Among the plains' best-known burrowing creatures are prairie dogs, gophers, swift foxes, and burrowing owls.

Filming in the plains was, for us, about the big picture and the small details. We wanted to capture the wide-open spaces, the dramatic changes in weather, and the sudden, terrifying storms. We also wanted to film the animal life that ranges from the continent's biggest land mammal, the bison, to its fastest, the pronghorn, and one of its smallest, the tiny jumping spider. Then there were the antics of the prairie dogs and prairie chickens, the resourcefulness of the swift foxes, and the surprising behavior of the bobcats—all of them making the plains, whether in blistering heat or freezing snow, home.

A bison's tail is often a handy warning flag. When it hangs down and is switching naturally, the animal is usually relaxed. If it extends out straight and droops at the end, it is becoming mildly agitated. If the tail is sticking straight up, they are ready to charge and you should be somewhere else.

BISON

The Great Plains once swarmed with bison—literally millions of them. The sight of these massive, shaggy beasts roaming the prairies is one of the most familiar and iconic images of North America.

Bison arrived across the Bering land bridge, from Asia and made the plains their home. For thousands of years, they roamed the land in vast herds with very little to fear, apart from the occasional wolf.

Until very recently, the bison was vitally important to the Plains Indians, who killed very few, and who used every single part of the animal, either for food or for warmth or tools. But the settlers, who arrived on the plains in the nineteenth century, killed bison in huge numbers, for food, for sport, and to deprive the Native Americans. Within a few years, over fifty million bison had been wiped out.

By the end of the nineteenth century, bison numbers were dangerously low, with just a few thousand left. Since then, efforts have been made to conserve them and to increase their numbers, and today there are about two hundred thousand bison.

Bison may be the largest and heaviest land animals in North America, but they are quick on their feet. With their small rumps and long front legs they can run up to forty miles (64 km) an hour. They feed on plains grasses, herbs, shrubs, and twigs. Like cows, they regurgitate their food and chew it as cud before digesting it.

Traditionally the bison's greatest enemy is the wolf, but these days they are not often in the same place together. In the lower forty-eight states, where most of the bison are, there are few wolves. But one place where they do coexist is the Wood Buffalo National Park in Alberta, the largest national park in Canada.

To record wolves chasing bison, we needed to film from a helicopter. Hunting is more likely at dusk and dawn, so each evening and again a few hours later in the early morning,

we flew over the park, following the bison. Every time we saw the herd unsettled, we knew it could mean a wolf was nearby—but it might mean a number of other things too, so there was nothing to do but wait patiently.

A shoot like this costs a huge amount and is unpredictable. You can put everything in place, with the best cameras and the most skilled cameraman or woman, and still not be in the right place at the right time. But after several days we got lucky—one evening a wolf pack appeared, and set off in pursuit of the herd.

The wolves were after a calf, but the bison mother, who only has one calf every couple of years, was not about to lose her offspring without a fight. The scene that followed was extraordinary, as the wolves cut the bison cow and calf off from the rest of the herd. At one point, a wolf had the calf's leg in its jaws and it seemed that all was lost. But the bison refused to give up. The calf kicked at the wolves and ran. The mother followed, coming between the wolves and her calf, until the two of them managed to rejoin the herd.

The hungry wolves sloped off. They would be back; they too needed to survive and had pups to feed. But we couldn't help being glad that this one brave mother and calf had escaped.

THE RUT

During the rut, or mating season from July to September, the males, who live in separate herds from the females and calves, will seek out females and battle with one another for "rights" to the cows.

Bison bulls can reach heights of over six feet (1.8 m) from hoof to shoulder and weigh up to two thousand pounds (907 k). They have heavy horns and a large hump of muscle that supports their enormous head and thick skull, a thick

mass of fur on their heads, and a heavy cape of fur even in summer. This enhances their size and protects them when they are fighting.

These great males can be truly impressive, and it's definitely not a good idea to get in their way when they are roaring and dueling with one another.

To film the confrontations, we needed to be able to follow them overland, so we mounted our camera on the back of a little ATV, put extra-wide tires on it, and waited for the action to start.

It was pretty nerve-wracking at times. Sitting in the front of the vehicle, our eye-level was lower than the bison's. We were looking up at them, and they looked enormous.

Keeping a careful distance, we filmed a number of bulls roaring, posturing, and intimidating one another by rolling their eyes. Then came the fight with two massive bulls crashing heads like battering rams, each trying to push harder than the other, snot and spit flying everywhere. The trick for us was to stay close, but not so close that they would plow into us. It was a dramatic scene as they fought, both reluctant to give up, until eventually there was a victor, who tossed his head and wallowed in the dirt to celebrate his triumph.

One in seven bison die each winter, but they don't die from cold; they die from starvation. Although they use their heads and hooves to move snow off vegetation, food is hard to find, and some, especially the younger calves, will perish.

The cold is their greatest threat, but it certainly isn't the only weather problem they have to face. The plains are the territory of sudden and violent storms, torrential rain, thundering hail, and the most terrifying weather phenomenon of all . . . tornadoes.

With each bull weighing more than two thousand pounds, the clash of fighting bison becomes one of the biggest collisions in nature.

Ninety percent of the world's tornadoes occur in North America, although tornadoes have occurred on every continent in the world except Antarctica.

TORNADOES

When the warm, moist air of the tropics comes up to meet the cold, dry air of the Arctic, right over the plains, it's a lethal mix, and the result can be a storm that rapidly evolves into a supercell, the most dangerous type of storm on the planet. In a supercell, there is a spinning updraft whirling at the center and generating downpours, flash floods, hail the size of baseballs, and most dangerous of all—tornadoes.

For animals caught in the path of a supercell, there is no choice but to ride out the storm and hope to survive. When a storm throws out huge black clouds and rotating winds, the prediction will always be trouble. And while not every supercell generates a tornado, many do.

While tornadoes have been seen in every state in the United States, the prairies are tornado country. The line down the center of the country, cutting through the Dakotas, Nebraska, Wyoming, Missouri, Kansas, Oklahoma, and Texas is known as "Tornado Alley." This is where, especially during the tornado season of April, May, and June, these dramatic and terrifying storms are frequent visitors. Between

eight hundred and eleven hundred a year, and sometimes more, batter the plains and the most destructive have enormous energy.

A tornado, also known as a twister, is a violently rotating column of air that is in contact with both the ground and the dense, towering cumulonimbus clouds above it. It looks like a funnel, surrounded by a swirling haze of dust and debris. Smaller tornadoes may measure only 250 feet (76 m) across, with wind speeds of little more than one hundred miles an hour (161 km), and may travel for a few miles and last only seconds before disintegrating. But large tornadoes can be as much as two miles (3.2 km) across, with wind speeds of three hundred miles an hour (483 km) and can travel for many miles, wreaking havoc in their paths.

Millions of North Americans live in the path of tornadoes and risk losing their homes, property, and even their lives every year. The deadliest tornado on record was in 1925, when the tri-state tornado killed a total of 695 people in Missouri, Illinois, and Indiana. The costliest was the Joplin tornado of May 22, 2011, which was a mile wide

with winds of up to two hundred miles per hour (322 km) and which struck the town of Joplin, Missouri, and caused damage estimated at $2.8 billion in addition to 160 deaths.

The large animals of the plains, like bison, can't outrun a tornado. All they can do is hope it passes them by. Some smaller animals can hide underground, but for others, it can be lethal; it is not unusual for smaller animals, both wild and domestic, to be picked up and dropped by the raging winds.

When we set out to follow a tornado, we wanted a different kind of footage. We wanted more than the shaky images that is all too often the result of trying to film a tornado on the move, usually through a car window. We wanted to film the story of the buildup to a supercell storm using a process called HDR—high dynamic range—that gives an intense image and a level of detail that is new and very exciting.

Even the experts can't tell you whether a particular storm will develop into a tornado. It's not an exact science so you play a waiting game as storms arrive and blow themselves out.

For this footage, we were joined by expert storm-chaser

Supercells are the most dangerous type of storm on the planet. In a supercell, there is a spinning updraft whirling at the center, and they generate downpours, flash floods, hail the size of baseballs, and most dangerous of all—tornadoes.

Roger Hill, who has chased after more than six hundred tornadoes and lived to tell the tale. Tornadoes tend to arrive in the late afternoon, and after studying the weather picture via satellite, Roger would give us the go-ahead if a storm was expected.

Watching a supercell sweep across the landscape is impressive and terrifying. Thunderous black clouds arrive at breakneck speed, charging toward us like a train. Following the storm is not easy. Driving through the core of one is a little like going through a carwash and a fairground ride all in one; you can't see out of the windows and the car is pushed so hard by the wind that you expect to flip over at any moment, while the hail can break the windshield.

On one day alone, during our filming, there were fourteen tornadoes in the area where we were, six people died, and a trailer park, a school, and a gas station had been flattened. We narrowly escaped and were very lucky.

PRONGHORN

Pronghorn are a unique species to North America. They are not goats or antelopes, although they are related to both, with their deerlike bodies, long snouts, and short tails. Like bison, seemingly endless numbers once covered the plains, stretching from Saskatchewan in Canada to just north of Mexico City. And like bison, they nearly became extinct. Populations declined from an estimated thirty million in the early 1800s, to less than 15,000 by 1915. Today, thanks to conservation efforts, there are once again around a million pronghorn roaming the plains.

They are graceful creatures. Both males and females have horns, though the females' tend to be much smaller, while the males' can be ten or twelve inches (25 to 30 cm) long. Unlike other hoofed creatures, their horns point backward, but it is the small forward-pointing prong on each horn that gives them their name. They have the only forked horns in the world, and the only ones that are shed every year (deer, moose, and elk shed their antlers, but antlers, which are bony projections, are not the same as horns which are predominantly skin and hair).

These beautiful long-legged creatures are born to run, and are the fastest land animals on the continent. They can keep up speeds of forty-five miles an hour (72 km) for prolonged periods, and can reach even faster speeds for short bursts. Their speed evolved to help them escape a single predator—the cheetah, which is the fastest land animal on earth. Cheetahs are now extinct in North America, but the pronghorn still use their speed to escape the wolves and coyotes since a pronghorn is an easier target than a bison.

Pronghorn are famed for their long migration. They follow the same routes year after year and one of the best-known is a route they have used for six thousand years, along a corridor that is less than 450 feet (137 m) wide in some places, traveling from the Grand Teton National Park to the Upper Green River Valley in Wyoming and back. This three-hundred-mile (483 km) round trip is second only to the caribou's trek for long-distance migration in North America.

PRAIRIE DOGS

Prairie dogs are the North American version of the meerkat. Members of the squirrel family, they are about the size of a rabbit and full of character, and like the meerkat, they will stand on their hind legs in order to scout for danger.

The most common of the five North American species are the black-tailed prairie dogs that inhabit the plains. They live in large communities in extensive networks of burrows and chambers known as "dog towns" that are marked by mounds of packed earth at their entrances.

Prairie dogs are among the most vital and significant of all prairie animals—more than any other creature, they hold the prairie ecosystem together. Many of the prairie's other animals and birds either depend on them as prey, or inhabit their disused burrows. The black-footed ferret, an endangered species, is entirely dependent on the prairie dog for survival.

Prairie dog burrows affect the type and quality of the surrounding vegetation. They build and rebuild the burrows,

The modern species of pronghorn is the only one to survive the Ice Age. Like the bison, the pronghorn came close to extinction, but today in the Great Plains states, there are up to a million.

Although they are rodents, prairie dogs were named dogs because of their bark-like calls. They have up to fifty different barks— thought to be the most complex language of any animal on earth apart from humans. The largest prairie dog town on record was in Texas, where it extended over 25,000 square miles (64,750 sq km) and was believed to be the home of 550 million prairie dogs.

from which so many other animals benefit, and there are listening posts near the exits, so that they can check on what's happening outside.

In the past, these networks of burrows reached for many miles over thousands of acres, but prairie dogs became the scourge of ranchers and many were poisoned or fumigated. Today the population is reduced, although there are still ten to twenty million prairie dogs in the United States. The largest remaining dog town is believed to be in South Dakota, and covers about 224 square miles (580 sq km).

Full of character and charm, the prairie dog families of a male, several females, and their young, will play together, groom one another, greet each other with a nuzzle, share food, and look out for one another. They also have a wide range of noises to warn other prairie dogs of different kinds of danger.

We spent several weeks camped out watching the prairie dogs from hides, or camouflage viewing areas, that we dug, which is the only way to watch animals on the plains where there is no cover, so that we could observe without disturbing them. It was impossible not to grow fond of them and to admire their intelligence, organization, family spirit, and comedy.

Their habit of celebrating the "all clear" after a predator has gone is especially amusing. Dozens of them will jump up and down giving a "yip, yip" all-clear call, a routine that's known as the jump-yip.

The most dramatic moment of our time with them came when a female prairie dog came face-to-face with a rattlesnake that was coiled at the mouth of the burrow where her pups were. All the other prairie dogs ran away, giving each other the call for "rattlesnake" as they went, but this brave mother fronted up to the snake in a dangerous but carefully calculated battle of wits. To stop it from entering the burrow, she darted forward, threatening to bite it, but always staying carefully out of range in case it struck at her.

When the stand off ended, it was the snake that gave in and moved away, while the prairie dog mother returned to her young and ushered them quickly underground.

Bobcats, which are found
only in North America, weigh
between eleven and thirty
pounds (5 to 14 kg) and are
roughly twice the size of the
average housecat. They live for
ten to twelve years and males
are bigger than females.

Bobcats have elegant pointed ears, like their relative, the lynx. They are fierce hunters and can kill prey bigger than themselves, pouncing up to ten feet (3 m).

BOBCATS

The chances of seeing a bobcat, North America's native wild cat, are pretty remote, unless you have a great deal of patience and a lot of luck. Like so many wild cats, they are shy, elusive, and difficult to spot.

These beautiful cats are members of the lynx family and are recognizable for their short bobtails, often just two inches (5 cm) long, which have black fur on top and a white underside. They have wide, flat faces with longer fur on the cheek area, long legs and big paws, and their color ranges from brown to brownish-red, with a white underbelly and black spots and bar markings that are more noticeable on its face, legs, and chest.

There are plenty of bobcats throughout the United States, southern Canada, and Mexico, so they are not endangered, but it is still unusual to see them. This is partly because people are just not used to spotting them. We found that when we first started looking for them, we didn't see any—but after a week spent learning to spot them, we saw plenty, sometimes several in a day.

We spent a few weeks watching bobcats and getting to know them, and found some of their behavior very similar to that of domestic cats. One bobcat in particular seemed almost to trust our two-man team and would allow us to walk with him for hours at a time. This cat had been chased off its territory by another cat and found itself in a more risky situation, so it may have been using us as a shield.

What was interesting was how close many people came to the bobcats in the national park without seeing them. Bobcats, like many other members of the cat family, like to use human paths and trails to avoid long grasses and irritants, such as ticks. Several times a bobcat would hear someone coming along the path and would flatten down at the side of the path while the person walked past, often just ten feet (3 m) away, unaware.

Like all cats, they are carnivorous, eating rabbits, birds, lizards, snakes, carrion, and—as we discovered—gophers. We watched one of the bobcats stalking gophers for several hours, with no success. The gophers keep their hind quarters inside the mouth of the burrow, so that they can slip back inside, and despite the bobcat's patient and stealthy ambush, the gophers were too quick. Finally, though, the bobcat succeeded, pouncing on an unsuspecting gopher that had its back to the cat. What followed was extraordinary—the bobcat threw the gopher in the air and jumped to catch it,

Bobcats don't just live on the plains; they are adaptable and can also be found in forests, deserts, swamps, and even suburban areas.

Swift foxes can run at speeds of up to thirty miles an hour (48 kph). Their average height is twelve inches (30 cm), and they live for three to four years.

not once but many times, in what looked like a celebratory dance. It was a moment of exuberance and playfulness that was a delight to see.

SWIFT FOXES

The swift fox is tiny; the size of a domestic cat, with huge pointed ears and a bushy tail. Though they are not endangered, the population in some areas where they were once abundant is fragmented and they can be hard to find.

A native of the Great Plains, the swift fox is, as its name implies, very fast, although it will spend more time in its underground den than any other member of the fox family.

Swift foxes are nocturnal and emerge from their dens to hunt rabbits, prairie dogs, squirrels, mice, birds, and other small creatures, as well as berries and seeds.

To film swift foxes, we once again dug hides several feet down to create a small area where we could remain concealed and observe and film them from eye level.

Our subjects were a family of swift foxes; a mom, a dad, and four playful cubs. In order to acclimatize them to our presence, we moved our hide a little closer every four or five days. It meant a lot of digging, which required pick-axes to get into the parched earth and resulted in a lot of blisters, but in the end, we were only about 20 feet (6 m) from this little family's den.

The cubs were growing fast and learning to hunt in preparation for independence. They practiced on bugs, frogs, grass, and just about anything that moved, under the tolerant eyes of their parents.

BURROWING OWLS

These amazing little owls that fly to the plains from Mexico, often take over disused prairie dog burrows, and we found a family that had set up home only a short distance from the swift foxes. It was not close enough, unfortunately, to use the same hides, so it was back to the digging. But once our hides were in place, we toted all our heavy camera equipment and set up camp in the hide to watch another set of parents raising their young.

The mother and father owls also had four young, and

Ferruginous Hawks

These large grassland hawks are the biggest ground-nesting birds in North America. The lack of trees on the plains means they build their nests on ledges, rocks, platforms, and on the ground, so their eggs and young are especially vulnerable to predators.

Ferruginous means "rusty color" and refers to the coloration of the bird's wing and legging feathers. They are members of the *Buteo* species, which is the Latin word for falcon or hawk.

They are so large that they are sometimes mistaken for eagles. Their wingspan is four to five feet (1.2 to 1.5 m) and as with all birds of prey, the females are bigger than the males. The hawks bond in pairs long-term and return to their familiar nesting grounds. The female will stay with the chicks for the first three weeks, and after that, both parents will hunt.

We had a difficult time finding Ferruginous Hawks to film. We wanted a nest with young birds in it, but the first nest we found contained two dead chicks. The adults will either not mate, or will abandon the nest if it is a poor year for food, and this seems to have been what happened. We put out a call among scientists and experts, and investigated another nine or ten nests before we found one on a rocky outcrop, where the parents were busy feeding three healthy chicks. It was very hot, and as the land baked under 115°F (46°C) heat for fifteen hours a day, the chicks wilted and suffered in their nest. Despite their mother's attempts to shelter them with her wings, they were utterly exposed and, very sadly, one of the chicks didn't make it.

Among the smallest owls in North America, burrowing owls, unlike other owls, are active during the day when they gather food for their young.

these four were learning to fly, running through the grass and flapping their wings before lifting off the ground for a second or two and then, more often than not, landing back down on one another's heads.

The male owl, a gorgeous specimen, would go off hunting for food for the whole family while the female, who looked a little worse for wear and whose hooked beak reminded us of Gonzo from the Muppets, watched the chicks.

The cooperation and care these owl parents showed their young was touching. The male would find a bug or a small rodent and bring it to the female, who would feed the chicks. Unlike many other birds of prey, there was no weakling who was ignored or pushed out. The four chicks were fed strictly in turn and all got the same amount of food.

Not only did the parents feed their young well but the male owl fought off a number of predators. Being on the ground, the chicks were vulnerable, but their dad wasn't about to let anything come near, and even when a large badger came along, he hurled himself at it in a ball of feathers and claws until the badger gave up and wandered off.

By the time the chicks were fully fledged, they were four very healthy specimens, and a testament to their parents' hard work and care.

PRAIRIE CHICKENS

The greater prairie chicken is a game bird, a member of the grouse family and, like so many other prairie species, it was once abundant throughout the plains areas but is now rare and endangered.

These are medium-sized stocky birds with rounded wings, striped brown and pale plumage, and short tails. The males have long, dark head feathers that can be raised or laid flat, and orange comb feathers over their eyes, as well as a bare orange neck patch.

Male prairie chickens indulge in an elaborate mating ritual called booming, in which they raise their head feathers, inflate their neck patches like little orange balloons, snap their tails, and stamp to impress the females. The booming noise they make, amplified by their air sacks, can be heard half a mile away. We wanted to film this, so we needed to find the booming grounds where the male prairie chickens spend up to two months displaying, before the dominant males do most of the mating.

When we found one in Kansas, we went several weeks

Male prairie chickens engage in elaborate mating rituals where their booming calls can be heard for over a mile, and they battle with others in special courtship areas known as "leks" to win the attention of the females.

before the prairie chickens were due to arrive, and dug holes in which we sank canvas hides. The idea was that when the prairie chickens arrived, they would get used to these hides, and we would then be able to film them without disturbing them.

During the booming season, we were able to slip into the hides each morning, while it was still dark. We would wait in the darkness for the birds to arrive at dawn, and as the sun rose, we were able to watch and film them for several hours.

The birds were so used to the hides that they treated them as part of the landscape. Sitting inside one of them, we would have male birds stamping on the canvas just above our heads, kicking up quite a racket.

Watching them through the fabric screen across the opening of the hide, as they puffed up their orange neck sacks and strutted for the females, they reminded us of little dinosaurs. We called them the Ninja chickens as they leaped in the air, attacking one another with their feet. They were fun to watch, and after a few days, it was easy to see which of the males was dominant and would be demanding most of the female attention.

JUMPING SPIDERS

We knew our film wouldn't be complete without a courtship ritual of a very different kind— but just as charming and funny. The jumping spiders are as small as a grain of rice, but they are lively, bright, and engaging little arachnids that proved to be more than worth the time we spent tracking them down and getting to know them.

Like all spiders, these little guys have eight eyes, but unlike many spiders, they have extremely acute eyesight, and they can jump more than fifty times their own body length. And when the males are out to impress the females, they crouch, bob, dance, and sing like something straight out of an animated movie.

While many spiders aren't that bright, the jumping spider is extremely smart—some

experts think they are as smart as domestic cats. In fact, when we started filming them, it was often as if they knew exactly what we wanted them to do.

Male jumping spiders have their work cut out for them. There's always a chance, a fairly significant one, that if the female doesn't like his attempts to woo her, she will simply eat him. So he goes in for an elaborate courtship ritual to entice her, performing a complex dance, while singing to her.

Our spiders kept us laughing the whole time—stunned at their ingenuity and bravado. The male sings by sending sound out from his rear end through his legs and into the surface he is on, then along and up the female's legs so that she feels it. It's an acoustic vibration that is not transmitted through the air. We used laser technology—the first time such a thing has been tried—to pick up the sound, and realized that our male was dancing in perfect time to his song and that the female was judging him on the song as well as the dance. Legs in the air, he gave it his all in a high-energy, high-octane performance that was beautiful to watch. At the end, we held our breath and were just as relieved as he was when she approved his efforts and accepted him as her mate.

LAST WORD

Who would have thought that those great open stretches of grassland held so many secrets and so much beauty? The animals of the plains are unique in being able to survive both the sizzling summers and the frozen winters with ingenuity and adaptability, and the creatures we got to know there enchanted us, surprised us, and filled us with respect for their ability to survive.

From the plains, the furthest point inland from the oceans, we moved both east and west, to the coasts where the climate, the wildlife, and the ecosystems were totally different, but just as absorbing and enlightening.

CHAPTER THREE

THE SAVAGE EDGE

The seas of North America remain an untamed wilderness of power, strength, and beauty, where a vast array of life explodes from the deep and some of the world's largest, most dangerous, and most unusual creatures are to be found.

North America's 150,000 miles (241,402 km) of coastline is the longest of any continent—and its two coasts could not be more different. On the East Coast, the land shelves gently into the sea, while on the West, steep cliffs create a sheer rock face that plummets into the depths.

These two vast oceans, the Atlantic on the East and the Pacific on the West, have little in common and are therefore home to very different species of marine wildlife. But while most species of animals on land are known, in the oceans of the world, there is still a huge amount to be discovered.

The story of the North American coasts is a story of two vibrant and dramatically contrasting worlds. And the key to these two worlds is a small and unique land barrier, the thirty-mile (48 km) Isthmus of Panama that joins Central America to South America and divides the oceans on either side. The very character of the East Coast, with its coral reefs, its Gulf Stream, and even its hurricanes, and of the West Coast, with its plummeting depths and rugged, rich nature, only persists because of this barrier and the diversion of currents which result. It is the greatest marine barrier on the planet, and has created the most diverse and magnificent coastlines in the world.

THE EAST COAST

On the East Coast, the seas are warmer and the tides play a crucial role. The vast stretches that are exposed with each receding tide were formed over millions of years, as the North American continent drifted west, leaving a flattened coastline in its wake. This has resulted in some of the largest tidal ranges on earth; in the Bay of Fundy, in Nova Scotia, the tide rises and falls by an astonishing forty feet, twice a day.

In the north, the East Coast curves around to Newfoundland, where the temperature remains below freezing for half the year, while down in the south, the Atlantic gives way to balmy waters and tropical temperatures. Once again, there is a huge difference, and these two extremes give life and sustenance to some very diverse marine life.

The Mesoamerican Barrier Reef is over five hundred miles (805 km) long and is the second largest in the world, after Australia's Great Barrier Reef.

THE CARIBBEAN: CORAL REEFS

In the tropics, the extensive shallows off the East Coast form a warm and inviting sea known as the Caribbean. In 1492, when Christopher Columbus discovered America, this was where he first landed, and he must have thought he had reached paradise.

In this region, the sun-warmed shallows provide the perfect conditions for one very special little animal: coral. Off the coast of Belize is a vast barrier reef that has a surface area of ten thousand square miles (26,000 sq km), stretches for over five hundred miles (805 km), and makes up 7 percent of the world's shallow coral reefs.

Reefs are made up of colonies of coral polyps, tiny living animals, whose stony outer skeletons band together to give coral reefs their rocky character. Although coral polyps are carnivorous and feed on small sea creatures that float by, extending tentacles to pull them in, most of their energy and nutrients come from tiny algae that live within the coral's tissue.

Reefs grow best in shallow, warm waters, and in the underwater oases that they create, there is more diversity of life than anywhere else in the Atlantic. They are home to hundreds of kinds of fish and small marine creatures that hide in the reef's rocky cliffs and clefts, including mollusks, worms, sponges, and crustaceans.

Among the myriad inhabitants of the reef, there are great shoals of the small silver fish known as silversides. They swim together in such huge numbers that they can appear to morph into one giant shape-shifting entity. But they have little defense against the tarpon, a large, scaly game fish which can be as much as eight feet (2.4 m) long, that will slip inside the shoal and strike from within, sucking up the silversides, one after another, in a giant feeding frenzy.

Tarpon, also known as sabalo real, cuffum, silverfish, and silverking, are unique and extraordinary fish. Fossils show that they are prehistoric and have survived unchanged for over one hundred million years. They owe this survival to their ability to adapt to different environments, and this, in turn, is due to their unique use of the swim bladder—an internal gas-filled sac—as a respiratory organ. While some other fish do have swim bladders, they are generally only to aid

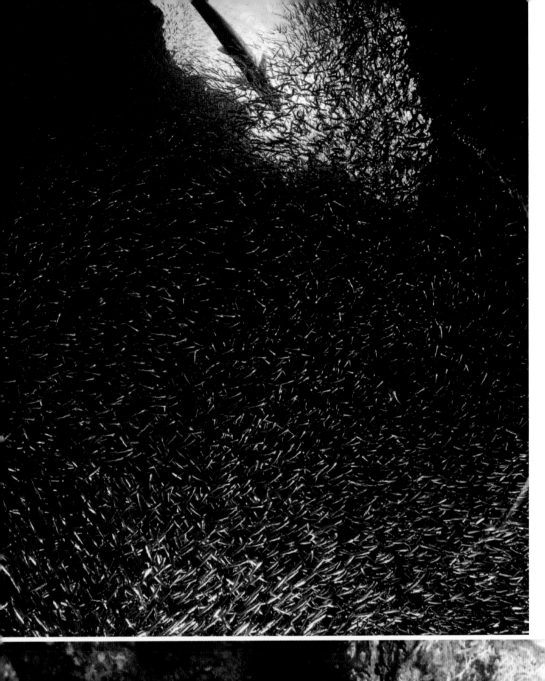

Florida is known as the shark attack capital of the world, with a yearly average of twenty-three shark attacks—more than any other place on earth. But few of Florida's shark attacks are fatal.

Hammerhead Sharks

The hammerhead shark's head is an amazing piece of anatomy built to maximize the fish's ability to find its favorite meal: stingrays. The shark's eye placement on each end of its very wide head, which can be up to five feet (1.5 m) wide, allows it to scan an area more quickly than other sharks can. It also has special sensors across its head that help it scan for food in the ocean. Living creatures' bodies give off electrical signals that are picked up by sensors on the prowling hammerhead. This helps it to find stingrays that hide under the sand on the seabed, and it uses its head to trap stingrays by pinning them to the seafloor. Hammerheads also eat crabs, squid, lobsters, and other sea creatures—including smaller sharks.

There are nine species of hammerhead, of which the great hammerhead is the largest. Unlike many other sharks, hammerheads give birth to live young, and the pups' heads are more rounded than their parents.

Despite their alarming appearance, hammerheads are seldom dangerous to man.

buoyancy, but in the tarpon, the swim bladder functions like a lung. They obtain air by rolling on the surface of the water and taking a gulp, and this ability means that tarpon can survive where other fish might not be able to, for instance, in fresh water and in oxygen-depleted, stagnant water. The young, in particular, can exist and mature in places where they can avoid predatory fish from reaching them.

The tarpon enjoy the warm Caribbean waters all summer long, but in winter, they head out to join the biggest migration of marine predators in North America, along with thousands of spinner and blacktip sharks. The whole army hitches a ride north on a giant current of warm blue water known as the Gulf Stream, and this leads them on a collision course with Palm Beach, on Florida's coastline.

FLORIDA: SHARKS AND HURRICANES

By late January, the sharks are streaming into the shallows around Palm Beach on Florida's panhandle, the strip of land on the southern tip, surrounded by sea on three sides.

Despite the heavily crowded beaches in this popular holiday region, few people are aware of the gathering masses of thousands upon thousands of sharks, just a short distance out to sea. Spinner sharks, sleek, and streamlined, can grow up to ten feet (3 m) long. Blacktips are similar but smaller, and both can leap out of the water and spin around several times. And while neither spinner sharks nor blacktips are man-eaters, they can and do bite, and they tend to get agitated if there's food around, so it's best to treat them with a great deal of respect.

Every year thousands of spinner sharks follow the Gulf Stream up Florida's coast, passing close to some of Florida's most popular beaches.

In the winter months in Florida, the spinners and blacktips lurk in the water and don't appear to be feeding or breeding; they just wait in these comfortable waters for spring, when they will become more active and head north into richer, temperate seas bursting with food.

But their pleasant wait is rudely interrupted when their most feared predator, the great hammerhead shark, arrives. Spinners and blacktips are minnows compared with these enormous sharks, which can reach lengths of over twenty feet (6 m) and can weigh over a thousand pounds (454 kg).

Great hammerheads appear in the shallows off Palm Beach each winter to feed on the smaller sharks, sending the spinners and blacktips into chaos as they strike out, using the maneuverability of their extraordinary flat heads and the 360-degree vision that their wide-set eyes give them.

As the temperature rises in the summer, the sharks move north, but at this time of year, Florida faces an even bigger threat than the sharks. At 80°F (27°C), the shallows of the Caribbean and the Gulf of Mexico reach a deadly tipping point. Water vapor fuels an already volatile atmosphere and when storms sweeping in off the Atlantic collide with this warm air, a hurricane—the deadliest force in nature—is born. Charged and violent, it begins to rotate, and while sea creatures can escape it in the depths of the ocean, on land there is no escape.

Every year, around seven hurricanes—some larger than the state of Florida—hurtle toward the East Coast of America and unleash hell. A big hurricane can force the ocean to surge twenty feet (6 m), causing devastating inland flooding. This is followed by winds of up to two hundred miles per hour (322 kph) that destroy everything in their path.

Filming a hurricane is not easy. There are obvious dangers, and the footage tends to be shaky and unclear. But we used the latest cutting-edge-technology cameras that can provide a stable image even when they are moving. And we headed into the biggest hurricane of 2011, Hurricane Irene, to show just what it's like to be in the center of a storm that can bend trees over double and hurl road signs, traffic lights, and even buildings to the ground. Shooting like this involves carefully calculated risk, and it can lead to some pretty hair-raising moments, but our crew emerged in one piece and with spectacular footage of the hurricane at its worst.

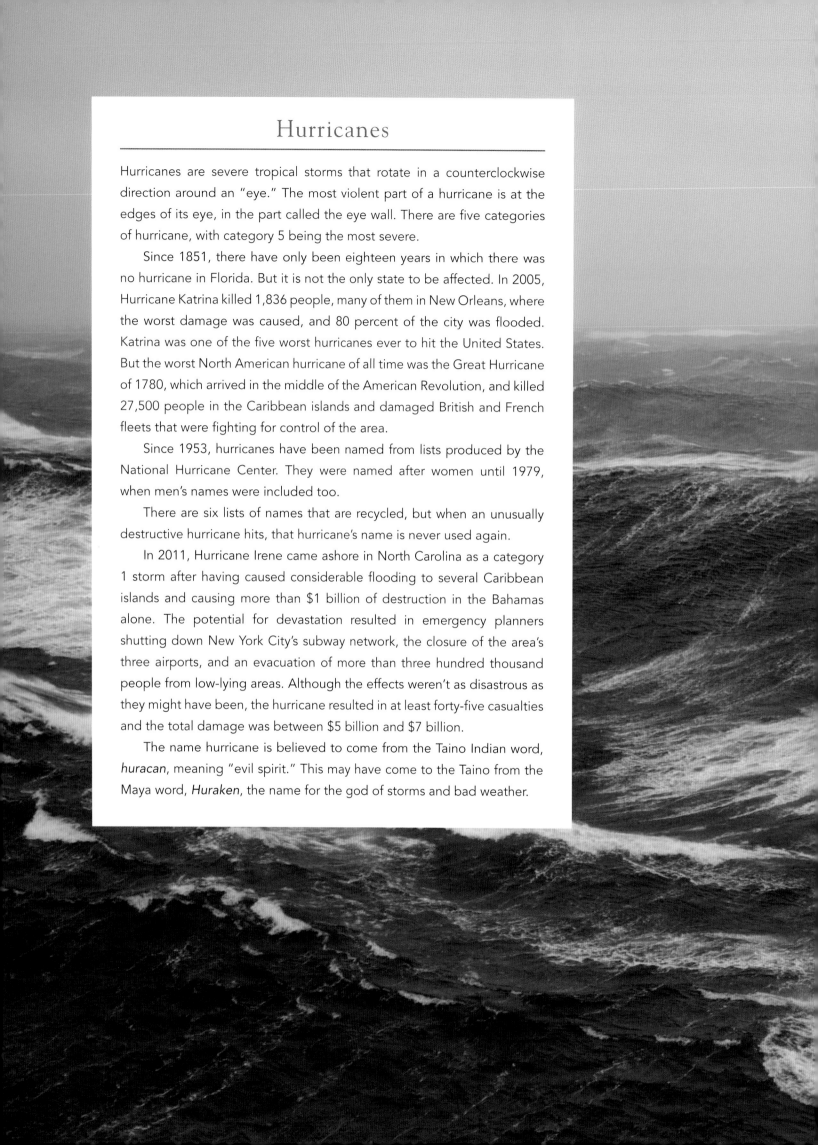

Hurricanes

Hurricanes are severe tropical storms that rotate in a counterclockwise direction around an "eye." The most violent part of a hurricane is at the edges of its eye, in the part called the eye wall. There are five categories of hurricane, with category 5 being the most severe.

Since 1851, there have only been eighteen years in which there was no hurricane in Florida. But it is not the only state to be affected. In 2005, Hurricane Katrina killed 1,836 people, many of them in New Orleans, where the worst damage was caused, and 80 percent of the city was flooded. Katrina was one of the five worst hurricanes ever to hit the United States. But the worst North American hurricane of all time was the Great Hurricane of 1780, which arrived in the middle of the American Revolution, and killed 27,500 people in the Caribbean islands and damaged British and French fleets that were fighting for control of the area.

Since 1953, hurricanes have been named from lists produced by the National Hurricane Center. They were named after women until 1979, when men's names were included too.

There are six lists of names that are recycled, but when an unusually destructive hurricane hits, that hurricane's name is never used again.

In 2011, Hurricane Irene came ashore in North Carolina as a category 1 storm after having caused considerable flooding to several Caribbean islands and causing more than $1 billion of destruction in the Bahamas alone. The potential for devastation resulted in emergency planners shutting down New York City's subway network, the closure of the area's three airports, and an evacuation of more than three hundred thousand people from low-lying areas. Although the effects weren't as disastrous as they might have been, the hurricane resulted in at least forty-five casualties and the total damage was between $5 billion and $7 billion.

The name hurricane is believed to come from the Taino Indian word, *huracan*, meaning "evil spirit." This may have come to the Taino from the Maya word, *Huraken*, the name for the god of storms and bad weather.

SOUTH CAROLINA: BOTTLENOSE DOLPHINS

These great Atlantic storms have helped to create the extensive salt marshes that can be found along the low-lying coast of the southern states. Fertilized by river sediment, this is exceptionally rich territory, and the murky waterways are filled with food for marine predators which include—astonishingly—the bottlenose dolphin.

At low tide, when the banks are exposed in South Carolina, these ingenious dolphins choose to head upriver, despite the very real risk that they could become stuck in the mud, because they have devised an extraordinary way of catching fish. Working in teams, they sweep the fish toward the bank, creating a bow wave to wash the fish onto the exposed mud bank. Then the dolphins throw themselves onto the bank and grab the flapping fish. It is a carefully orchestrated operation—the further up the bank they go, the better the chance of catching fish, and the greater the likelihood that they will be stranded. But they know what they're doing; they even land on their right sides on the bank, coordinating with one another to avoid colliding.

This extreme fishing technique has been mastered by fewer than one hundred dolphins, and the knowledge is passed down from generation to generation as a remarkable testament to their teamwork and intelligence.

DELAWARE BAY: HORSESHOE CRABS

The horseshoe crab is the oldest animal on the planet, a living fossil unchanged for 450 million years. With ten legs, two complex eyes and several simple ones, and a tail that acts like a rudder, it's a strange looking creature. In fact, the horseshoe crab is not really a crab at all. Like crabs, it's an anthropod but horseshoe crabs are most closely related to spiders and scorpions.

Delaware Bay, on the northeast seaboard of the United States, is where the largest concentration of these ancient creatures can be found. When the tide is at its highest during the nesting season, hundreds of thousands of them emerge from the water onto the beach to mate and lay their eggs.

The larger and stronger females head for the high water mark, while several males, using a specially developed appendage to clasp the female, cling on from behind, fighting each other for dominance.

The females produce about 80,000 eggs each year, and once they are fertilized she buries around 4,000 to 5,000 in the sand, returning again and again until all her eggs are buried. Eventually there are more than 1,000,000 miniature crabs growing beneath every square foot of beach.

So how has this fascinating creature survived unchanged for so long? The key to its endurance lies in three special

Each spring, on the highest tides, thousands of horseshoe crabs come ashore to lay their eggs.

features: First, its hard, curved shell makes it a difficult target for predators; second, it can survive for up to a year without food; and third, it can withstand extreme temperatures.

While most predators can't get under the horseshoe's shell, their eggs are far more vulnerable, especially to birds. When horseshoe crabs first roamed the oceans, there were no birds, which is probably why burying their eggs out of the water was such a good idea. But today, a million shore birds like sandpipers and the red knot depend on the eggs to fuel their winter migration, scooping up the dead eggs lying on the surface that have been disturbed by the arrival of fresh waves of horseshoes.

Delaware Bay is the largest staging area for shorebirds migrating from South America up to their Arctic breeding grounds. The birds have a two- to three-week stopover to replenish their energy supplies by feeding on the horseshoe eggs and will rapidly gain weight at this stage to fuel the rest of their journey.

The horseshoe crab's other predator is man. Adult crabs are caught to use as fishing bait and this has had a devastating impact on crab numbers in recent years.

NEWFOUNDLAND: MURRES AND HUMPBACK WHALES

Moving on up the East Coast, you arrive at Newfoundland, in

the far north, where the temperature can be below freezing for half the year. But though it is bitterly cold, this area is where the Gulf Stream mixes with Arctic currents and generates an explosion of life, providing the greatest riches on the East Coast. It was once said that the cod in these waters were so dense that fishermen could walk across their backs. What is left today is just a fraction of the great shoals of the eighteenth century, but the area still attracts huge numbers of animals and birds because of the variety of fish still available.

Every year, millions of nesting seabirds descend on a tiny, rocky outcrop called Funk Island, thirty-seven miles (60 km) northeast from Newfoundland. This little island is home to the largest bird colony in North America. Its name refers to the bad odor there, the result of the huge deposits of guano left by the birds.

Murres, also known as flying penguins, are among the ten or more species of seabirds that nest there. The murres only return to land to breed, and their chicks are raised to coincide with the arrival of one particular little fish—the capelin. Every summer, massive shoals of capelin rise from the depths, driven by their instinct to spawn. These seas were once home to huge numbers of cod, which drew fishermen from around the world. After eight million tons of cod were caught in just fifteen years the fishing industry here collapsed. Capelin are

Humpbacks whales are the fifth largest animal in
the world. They get their name from the hump
on the forward part of the dorsal fin and the way
they arch their backs before they dive.

the main food of cod, and when the cod disappeared, capelin numbers rose.

Another visitor to the cold seas of the North Atlantic is the humpback whale. Dozens of these thirty-ton (27,000 kg) giants make the thirty-six-hundred-mile-long (5,794 km) journey from their breeding grounds in the Caribbean, where the water is warm but nutrient-poor, to these abundant waters for a three-month-long feeding event. The food they eat now will last them for months when they travel back down south, so there's no time to lose, and with every lunge, the humpback gulps down a ton of capelin. Only coasts as rich in food as this one can support whales in such numbers.

It's hard to imagine that once the whales and the seabirds have had their fill, there would be any capelin left. But those

that survive swim on and head for the shore, where they throw themselves as high up the beach as possible, to spawn. They have just minutes to pair up, mate, and get back to the sea before they die; a hazardous ritual that inevitably ends in suffocation for some of the males and females. So why do they do it? The answer is that their fertilized eggs stand a far greater chance of survival away from marine predators.

Sea surface temperatures in the tropical Atlantic are rising over the long-term, driven in part by the rising concentration of greenhouse gases and this likely will result in more frequent tropical storms and hurricanes.

Although murres, with their black-and-white feathers and upright stance, look very similar to penguins, the two are not actually related. The murre is from the Auk family of birds.

Every summer, massive shoals of capelin rise from the depths, driven by their instinct to spawn.

THE WEST COAST

As the continent drifted west into the Pacific plate millions of years ago, the coastline was forced upward, creating mountains and high cliffs that plummet into the ocean depths. Beside this dramatic and rugged coast lies the Pacific Ocean, a sea even more bountiful than the Atlantic, and so big that you could fit the entire world's landmass into it and still have room for another Africa.

Bordering the ocean is a mountain range, starting with the Rocky Mountains and running down the entire West Coast. And this mountainous coastline generates some of the most astonishing sights in the world. This is the home of Mavericks in San Francisco, one of the biggest surf breaks in the world, with giant waves produced when ocean swells from across the Pacific hit the steep-sided bay. It is also the home of the billions of microscopic plankton that phosphoresce in huge numbers with a dazzling electric-blue light.

Along the Southern California coast is one of the most amazing of all marine habitats: the kelp forest. From above the water, this may look like huge mats of floating brown seaweed, but under the surface, there is a mysterious world that is home to a myriad of creatures; fish, invertebrates, algae, marine birds, and mammals, all of them dependent on the towering forests of giant kelp that cling to the coast.

From Canada to California, the cool deep-sea currents of the Pacific serve up a constant supply of food from the depths. And this plankton soup feeds walls of giant invertebrates carpeting the underwater cliff faces, where ancient anemones grow to three feet tall and shelter communities of oddities, such as the grunt sculpin, a crawling miniature fish that takes refuge in a discarded barnacle shell.

Some plankton produce a ghostly blue phosphorescence when disturbed, but this distress flare can also be set off by the tumbling surf, as seen here.

The killer whale, or orca, with ten tons of pure power, is the only predator capable of taking on a large whale.

THE ALEUTIANS: COASTAL BEARS AND WHALES

At the very top of the Pacific coast, off of Alaska and marking the line between the Pacific Ocean and the Bering Sea, lies a chain of volcanic islands known as the Aleutians. In the summer, the coastal waters here are even richer than those around Newfoundland. But in early spring, after the Alaskan winter, times are still hard.

On these shores, coastal brown bears, straight out of hibernation, are surviving on their last fat reserves. Food

is on its way, but they must wait. The older bears rest to conserve their strength, while the far more lively cubs roll around and play.

In early May, gray whales appear offshore after migrating north from Pacific lagoons along the Baja Peninsula in northwest Mexico, an area where huge numbers of whales, including gray, humpback, sperm, finback, minke, and even blue and orca are regularly seen.

When the gray whales appear around the Aleutians, the bears become more alert. This is their lifeline, but they

can't reach the whales themselves; they must rely on others to help out. And help is at hand, because the bears aren't the only ones waiting for the gray whales. As the new arrivals pass through the narrow bottlenecks between the islands, especially in the Isanotski Strait, or False Pass, as it's known locally, there are killer whales lying in ambush.

The killer whale, or orca, is ten tons of pure power—the only predator capable of taking on a large whale. Orcas hunt everything from fish to seals, penguins, squid, sea turtles, sharks, and even other kinds of whales. At the top of their list are gray whale calves. The killer whales like to feast on the calves' nutritious tongues and soft flesh, and this is one of their favorite West Coast hunting grounds. They are clever predators and will chase the mother and calf, sometimes for hours, until the mother is exhausted and the calf is separated from its mother's side and drowned.

Once the killer whales have feasted, much of the rest of the carcass will eventually wash ashore. The whale blubber is what the bears have been waiting for; it provides a high-energy meal that keeps the bears going until food is more plentiful.

The Aleutian Islands are part of Alaska, and therefore the United States. The fourteen large and fifty-five small islands contain fifty-seven volcanoes and are part of the Pacific mountain system. It is believed that they may have formed the land bridge to Russia, across which the first humans entered North America. The native people are the Aleut.

Unlike most whales, killer whales, have teeth and are actually a kind of dolphin. They are the largest of all dolphins. They are most common in Arctic and Antarctic waters. They can live to be as old as ninety, and their only enemies are humans.

The peregrine falcon mates
for life. Here are a male and
female sharing food.

CALIFORNIA: PEREGRINE FALCONS AND SPINNER DOLPHINS

At the top of the mountainous world of the West Coast is North America's most extreme aerial predator. More numerous here on the cliffs of the West Coast than anywhere else on the continent, the peregrine falcon's weapon is her extreme speed.

The falcon we filmed was a mother with two hungry chicks waiting back in her nest, which was high up in a niche in the cliffs. The chicks need to feed twice a day, so the mother had to leave them alone while she hunted for food, homing in on migrating shorebirds or, in one case, a solitary mourning dove. The peregrine falcon will catch its prey in midair, swooping before the other bird even knows what's happening.

The mother returned to the nest with her catch, tearing it apart to feed her chicks. But the inaccessibility of the nest, over one hundred feet (30.5 m) up the cliff face, was not enough to keep the chicks safe when she was away. Snakes such as the gopher snake were frequently scaling the sheer rock to try to snatch a chick and the mother falcon was constantly on the alert, fierce and protective in her efforts to safeguard her chicks.

In a remarkable scene, she spotted a gopher snake and swooped to attack it, lunging at it until it fell dramatically from the cliff to the rocks below. The snake was a very real threat, but the mother falcon had zero tolerance for anything that came within range of her nest, whether it was a threat or not. Even innocent passersby, like a group of brown pelicans, each of them ten times her size, were dive-bombed by her over and over again until they fled.

A long way south of California, the shallow continental shelf extends far out to sea and the spinner dolphins, which feed in the deep waters along the edge of it, patrol forty miles off the shores of Costa Rica, where families merge into a superpod up to five thousand strong in order to ward off killer whales and sharks.

Spinner dolphins are the acrobats of the oceans, leaping out of the water and spinning in the air before landing back in the water. Their exuberance, energy, and ability are thrilling to watch, but no one really knows why they do it. Is it to communicate with other dolphins? Or perhaps to shed parasites? Or for physiological reasons, such as keeping their body temperature regulated, or ejecting water from the upper respiratory tract? Or perhaps it really is for the

Peregrine falcons are the fastest creature on the planet, reaching speeds close to two hundred miles per hour (322 kph). They typically attack at dawn or dusk and capture their prey with their sharp talons in mid-air.

sheer joy of it? No one truly knows.

Just before we began filming these bright and entertaining mammals, an oil survey boat decided to do some sonar testing right on the spot where the dolphins regularly gather. The boat scared them off and we were concerned that the shoot might fail, but we did eventually find them.

We were on a fairly small fishing boat, and on the way back to our base we got caught in a huge squall with rain, thunder, and lightning flashing down on us and churning the seas. We had to head rapidly to shore, thankful that we had made it in one piece.

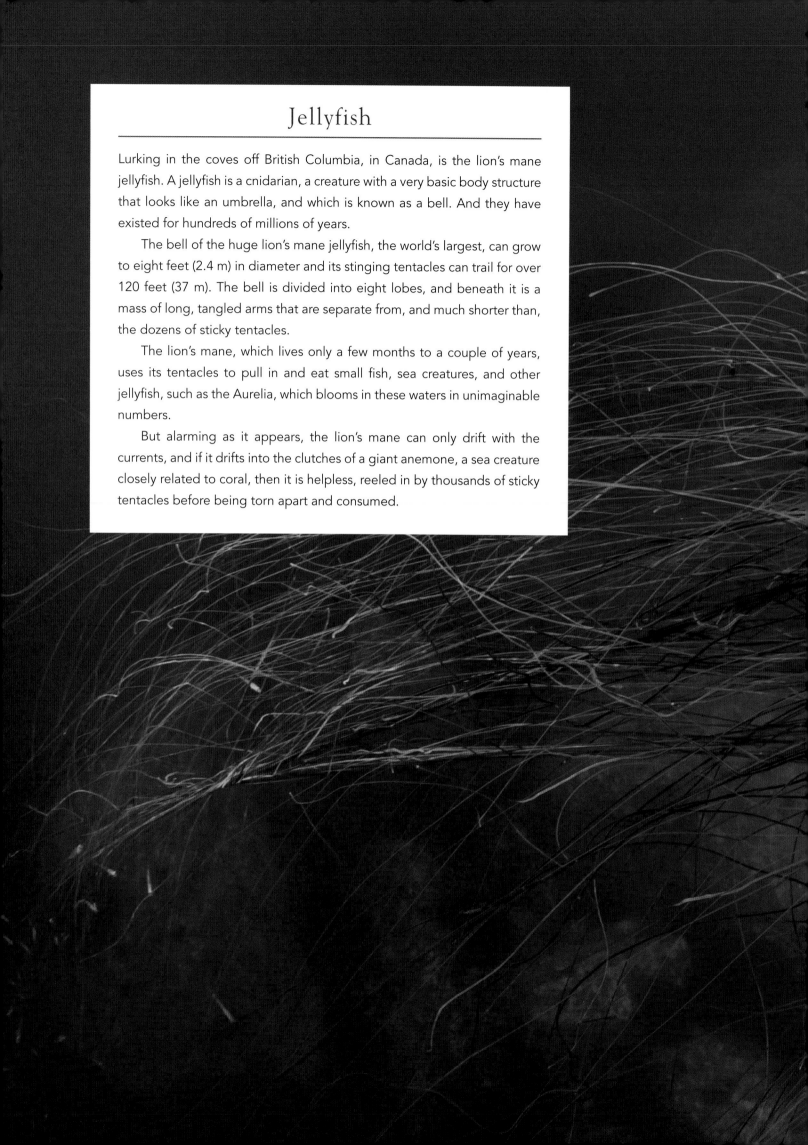

Jellyfish

Lurking in the coves off British Columbia, in Canada, is the lion's mane jellyfish. A jellyfish is a cnidarian, a creature with a very basic body structure that looks like an umbrella, and which is known as a bell. And they have existed for hundreds of millions of years.

The bell of the huge lion's mane jellyfish, the world's largest, can grow to eight feet (2.4 m) in diameter and its stinging tentacles can trail for over 120 feet (37 m). The bell is divided into eight lobes, and beneath it is a mass of long, tangled arms that are separate from, and much shorter than, the dozens of sticky tentacles.

The lion's mane, which lives only a few months to a couple of years, uses its tentacles to pull in and eat small fish, sea creatures, and other jellyfish, such as the Aurelia, which blooms in these waters in unimaginable numbers.

But alarming as it appears, the lion's mane can only drift with the currents, and if it drifts into the clutches of a giant anemone, a sea creature closely related to coral, then it is helpless, reeled in by thousands of sticky tentacles before being torn apart and consumed.

A spinner dolphin can leap
fifteen feet high (5 m) and spin
for up to seven rotations.

THE SEA MOUNT: MORAY EELS AND LEATHER BASS

Far out in the open ocean, which can be several miles deep, there are oases known as seamounts. These seamounts are the tops of underwater mountains, which reach from the depths to just under, or sometimes even above, the surface of the water. Sometimes as much as a mile wide, they are shallow areas filled with nutrient-rich plant life. Fish and other sea creatures are drawn to them to feed, and it was on one of these mounts that we were able to film an extraordinary alliance for the first time.

The moray eel is normally a shy, solitary, nocturnal hunter with bad eyesight. But on a seamount 250 miles (402 km) off the coast of Panama, we had heard the moray eels form a partnership with another solitary creature, the leather bass. The three-foot-long (1 m), three-pound (1.4 kg) leather bass are too big and bulky to catch the little fish hiding in the nooks of the coral reef, so the moray eels, which can penetrate deep inside the corals, with their six-foot-long (2 m) tapering

bodies, flush them out—and into the mouths of the waiting leather bass. And the morays have the advantage of protection from the leather bass.

This unusual partnership known as shadow hunting is found on seamounts, and is believed to occur because of their extreme isolation. And although it has been known about for some time, it has never before been filmed. So assistant producer Jonathan Smith set out to see if it was possible, and the trip turned out to be quite an adventure.

Jonathan set off with legendary underwater cameraman Didier Noirot who worked for many years with world-famous French underwater filmmaker Jacques Cousteau, until his death in 1997. We knew that if anyone could capture this unique underwater relationship, it would be Didier.

After flying to Panama and a six-hour taxi journey, they arrived at the boat that was to take them out to sea—a catamaran, moored several miles upriver, deep into the jungle. They woke the next morning to monkeys swinging through the trees above their heads. After another six-hour journey, this time downriver, they reached the sea and for the

next four days they headed west, through appalling weather and wild seas, until they reached the seamount. They only had ten days to get their footage.

They planned to spend as much time as possible underwater, wearing rebreathing equipment, or a closed-circuit underwater breathing apparatus. A rebreather recirculates the exhaled gas for reuse and does not discharge it to the atmosphere or water. In other words, there are no bubbles to distract the fish, and you can stay underwater for much longer periods than with ordinary scuba equipment.

They may have had great equipment and the world's best underwater cameraman, but the weather was not on their side. For eight days they were battered with big seas and wild winds. It was extremely difficult just getting themselves

and their kit into the dive boat, and despite spending four to five hours underwater each day, they couldn't find what they were looking for.

On their last day, the shout came up from one of the two diving guides who had gone along. The eels and the bass were there, working together, just as they had hoped. They got underwater as fast as they could. There was a lot to do in that short time—they needed close-ups, wide shots, long shots, and plenty of detail, and they had no idea how long they might have. In the end, the whole event lasted just twenty-three minutes before the eels and bass went their own ways. But it was enough; Didier shot some extraordinary footage of this unique cooperation and back on the boat, they enjoyed a great celebratory breakfast before beginning their four-day journey back to the shore.

CHAPTER FOUR

LEARN
YOUNG
OR DIE

The Rocky Mountains
stretch from British
Columbia in western
Canada, to New Mexico
in the southwest states,
a distance of over 3,000
miles (4,830 km).

Running down the west side of North America is one of the longest mountain chains on Earth, the Pacific American Cordillera, that stretches for 4,350 miles (7,000 km) from Alaska through Canada, and down through the Rocky Mountains of the United States, to the Sierra Madre in Mexico. This chain, made up of many mountain ranges, continues on into the Andes of South America, forming the longest series of mountain chains in the world.

The origin of the Pacific American Cordillera was the collision between the Pacific and American plates sixty-five million years ago, pushing up a series of mountain ranges along the coast of North America in a north-south direction.

The only mountains on the east side of North America are the Appalachians, the oldest mountains on the continent, formed about 450 million years ago, and now eroded by age into gentler slopes. They contrast with the much higher jagged peaks of the Rocky Mountains and the Alaska Range, which includes Denali, or Mount McKinley, the tallest mountain in the world, when measured from base to summit.

The amazing length of the Pacific American Cordillera means that every type of landscape and habitat is present somewhere, from the tropical peaks of Costa Rica, to the permanently glacier-covered mountains of Alaska. On many of North America's mountains, seasons are short and weather can change from summer to winter in hours. And weather isn't the only powerful force to shape these peaks. All along the Pacific American Cordillera there are geological hotspots where volcanic activity can be seen, and in places, these peaks are still growing, thrust upward by the continuing seismic and volcanic activity of the colliding plates. The Sierra Nevada in California is growing at a rate of a third of an inch per year; and Alaska's Mount Redoubt, in the Aleutian Range, is sleeping under a lava plug; while Yellowstone is the top of an active supervolcano—if it erupted, it would be the biggest natural disaster in the history of mankind. Further south, Mexico's Popocatepetl Volcano, which sits halfway between Mexico City and the city of Puebla, blasted a tower of ash over nearby towns and villages in 2012, prompting fears of a full-scale eruption that could affect the twenty-five million people who live within a sixty-mile (97 km) radius.

The mountains are wild, unpredictable, dramatic, and, at times, terrifying and to live in these conditions, animals have to be highly adapted and resourceful. They must learn while young to compete for food and shelter or they will die. Only a handful of hardy creatures will venture to the higher slopes and the pressure to survive can lead to titanic struggles.

MOUNTAIN WEATHER

The Pacific American Cordillera's north-to-south orientation, and the lack of any east-to-west mountain ranges, means there is no barrier to cold air from the arctic or warm air from the south. Likewise, weather on the eastern side can be very different to that on the west.

On the west side of the range, in winter, moist air masses flood in from the Pacific, while cold continental air masses pour down from the arctic along the eastern front of the Rockies, like water escaping from a dam. These air masses can lower January temperatures to -50°F (-46°C). The arctic air is bone dry and sometimes crests the mountain ridges, spilling over onto the west side. Because this air is so dense and cold, it rides under the moist pacific clouds, pushing them higher. The mix creates fierce blizzards with one hundred-mile-per-hour (161 kph) winds and heavy snow. But where winter storms are channelled through high passes in the mountains, the airflow becomes faster, meaning that the valleys directly below these passes often have less winter snowfall than other areas. This is called the Venturi effect.

As the snow piles up on the mountain slopes, avalanches become a major hazard. Warm weather after heavy snowfall can mean that the fresh snow doesn't always bond to the frozen, hard-packed layers beneath. As the weight builds, cracks form high on the east face of the mountains and if the angle of the slope is greater than thirty degrees, the snow will begin to slide. An avalanche can reach speeds of over eighty miles (129 km) per hour in just five seconds, becoming a wall of death that can splinter trees like matchsticks and destroy all in its path.

With the arrival of the polar winds, winter on the eastern slopes of the northern Rockies is one of the coldest on the planet. But occasionally and abruptly this changes in the spring, as the temperature rises rapidly and deep snow disappears without a trace of melt water. The Athabaskan Indians called this dramatic temperature rise the Chinook or "snow eater." The greatest recorded temperature change in twenty-four hours was caused by Chinook winds on January 15, 1972, in Loma, Montana, where the temperature rose from -56°F (-49°C) to 49°F (9°C). But while the sudden rise in temperature can provide relief from the cold for both people and animals, temperatures plummet again once the phenomenon has passed.

There are more than 100,000 avalanches a year in North America. A large avalanche can release 8.8 million cubic feet (250,000 cu m) of snow.

WRANGELL-ST. ELIAS

At the far northern end of the American mountain chain lies the intersection of four major mountain ranges: Wrangell, Chugach, St. Elias, and the Alaskan mountain ranges. These are the ultimate in mountains, creating one of North America's last true wildernesses.

Alaska is the largest of the fifty states and is situated in the far northwest of the American continent, with Canada on its eastern side, and the Arctic and Pacific Oceans surrounding it. Divided from Russia only by the Bering Strait, it has the fourth lowest population of any state. Over half the population of just under 723,000 people live in the area of the largest city, Anchorage, while the state capital, Juneau, has a population of only thirty thousand, and is so remote that it can only be reached by plane or ferry.

A few hundred miles north of Juneau, Mount St. Elias stands at the border of the Wrangell-St. Elias National Park and Preserve, the largest in the United States. The park contains nine of America's sixteen tallest mountains and

covers an area of 20,500 square miles (53,095 sq km), a region bigger than New Jersey, Connecticut, and Massachusetts combined.

On the other side of the park boundary stands Mount Logan, the second highest mountain in North America, and with the largest base circumference of any nonvolcanic mountain in the world. At 19,551 feet (5,959 m), active tectonic plate uplifting means it is still rising in elevation.

More than two hundred glaciers, some as large as sixty miles (97 km) wide, creep across this landscape, including the three largest in North America. It's the greatest area of ice outside the Polar Regions; a land still trapped in the Ice Age.

These mighty ice fields are so thick they have buried mountains, leaving only the isolated summits, like rocky islands, to poke through. Surrounded by permanent ice, these peaks are called nunataks and summer here is one of the shortest on the continent, lasting just one month.

It's hard to believe that anything could survive here but there is one tough little animal that calls the nunataks

Alaska contains over half the world's glaciers and seventeen of the twenty highest peaks in the United States.

Like pikas, marmots live in mountainous areas like the Cascades, Rockies, and Sierra Nevada mountains.

At 19,551 feet (5,959 m) Mount Logan in Yukon, Canada, is the tallest mountain in Canada and the second tallest in North America behind Mount McKinley.

home and you can hear its chirping call echo across the white wilderness. The collared pika is a small, furry mammal, with rounded ears and no tail. It looks like a mouse, and is not much bigger, but is actually related to rabbits and hares.

Pikas live on rocky mountainsides and can withstand the cold—they don't hibernate so they need enough food to last through the long winter, and they spend the short summers in a frenzy of activity, collecting summer flowers, grasses, shrubs, twigs, and lichen for their stores. Mouths stuffed full, they race back and forth all day to their rock crevice homes to add to their growing stockpile, taking only short breaks between shifts. To see them through the winter, they must collect fifty times their own body weight in vegetation.

Until recently, they were believed to be solely herbivores. But a recent discovery changed that. Dead migratory birds have been found collected in the pika's piles of vegetation. It seems the pika store dead birds that they find and eat their

brains to supplement their winter diets.

Even with the birds to eat, finding food on these isolated peaks is hard and competition is fierce. Pikas give birth to up to five young, which must then find their own territories and strike out over the glaciers and ice fields to find new nunatuk islands to colonize.

For our pika footage, a team of three camped on a glacier in the ice-field mountains of the St. Elias range for three weeks. Dropped off by helicopter, they had a satellite phone in case of emergency, but otherwise they were on their own with a tent and a lot of ice. With twenty-two hours of sunlight each day, there was plenty of time for spotting pikas, though they can be elusive little creatures because they are so small, and scurry from one rock crevice to another. The team was lucky because despite the chill of the ice, the sun was shining—though the glare from the ice was dazzling—and it was surprisingly warm.

The pika is sometimes known as the "whistling hare" because of its high-pitched alarm call. While they are solitary animals, they live in densely packed colonies and spend the summer in a frenzy of activity collecting enough food to see them through the long winters.

DENALI (MOUNT McKINLEY)

Not far from Mount St. Elias is the most spectacular Alaskan mountain of all—Mount McKinley, now more commonly known as Denali (the high one), is the tallest mountain in the world. While Mount Everest is at a higher elevation, measuring from sea level, it is actually only 18,000 feet (5,486 m) from base to tip. Denali, at 20,320 feet (6,194 m) is more than two thousand feet taller.

The peak of Denali is covered by clouds for 70 percent of the year, so to fly over it on a clear day is very lucky, and simply breathtaking. It stands in its own National Park, six million acres of wilderness, bisected by a single road. On the lower slopes, there are alpine meadows where, in the short summer season, grizzly bears can devour two hundred thousand berries a day before returning to the higher peaks to hibernate.

These grizzlies are found right across the Alaskan mountains. They hibernate in mountain dens and as spring approaches, they make the perilous journey down the snow-laden slopes, mother bears leading their new cubs, to the meadows and forests where they will stock up on tubers and berries.

But above the meadows, Denali is an arctic desert devoid of life. The scale of the landscape here is vast; the sheer walls of the Great Gorge measure nine thousand feet (2,743 m) deep—that's three thousand feet (914 m) deeper than the Grand Canyon, though the Great Gorge is filled with four thousand feet (1,219 m) of glacier, so unlike the Grand Canyon, it isn't all exposed.

Humans are the only ones to venture into this extreme place. To climb the mountain takes ten days and five overnight camps, and it's a technically difficult snow and ice climb that can only be undertaken by experienced climbers. This is the remotest and highest point on the American continent. But it's only possible to climb Denali during the summer months. In winter, the hurricane force winds drive the temperature as low as -118.12°F (-83.4°C), the lowest temperature ever recorded in North America. Nothing can survive here; with its extreme height and it subarctic position, Denali is perhaps the coldest mountain on the planet.

THE NORTHERN LIGHTS

In the most northern latitudes of Canada and Alaska, a hundred miles (161 km) beyond Denali, it is possible to see one of the natural wonders of the world. The Aurora Borealis, or Northern Lights, is a luminous display of shimmering colors that dance across the night sky in regions of the world close to the North Pole. Viewing the Aurora from any distance is special, but to experience the true magic of this natural phenomenon, you need to get as close as possible. Assistant producer Nick Lyon took up the challenge, and set out to film the Aurora from the observatory at the University of Alaska in Fairbanks.

Fairbanks is seven hundred miles (1,127 km) or so north of Juneau, on the edge of the Arctic Circle—the circle of latitude that encompasses all the Arctic regions around the North Pole, and which runs right through Alaska from east to west, including the northern third of the state. Nick had hoped to get some dramatic footage from the observatory, but decided to set out by car to get even closer to the Aurora by traveling into the Arctic Circle.

Nick and a colleague set out along the road to Prudhoe Bay, which is on the far northern coast of Alaska. There's an oilfield there, and the only traffic on the ice-bound road were the heavy trucks heading up to the base.

It was -10°F (-23.3°C) inside the car and -40°F (-40°C) outside—so cold that their beards froze. At these temperatures, a sharp breath in could literally knock them over as the iced air entered their lungs. They didn't dare turn off the engine in case it seized up, and the plastic cable on their camera froze so hard it would have snapped in two if they'd tried to bend it. The snow was waist-deep, and when they got out of the car, they sank into it. It was wolf territory and although wolves don't usually hunt man, in the darkness, half buried in the snow, they began to feel just a little worried. But all that was forgotten when they saw the Northern Lights—they lit up the whole sky in a stunning show of greens and blues, swirling in breathtaking and unforgettable ribbons and bows.

Aurora Borealis
The Science
Behind the Magic

The Northern Lights or Aurora Borealis is named after Aurora, the Roman goddess of dawn, and Boreas, the Greek name for the north wind. It is made up of discharged particles from the sun that pass through the magnetic shield of the Earth and enter the Earth's atmosphere. As they do so, they mix with atoms and molecules of nitrogen and oxygen gasses and it is this combination that creates the dazzling multicolored lights that can be seen from the ground.

The particles from the sun—also made up of gasses—take two to three days to travel the ninety-three million miles (150 million km) through space to reach the Earth. The sun's particles are magnetically charged and are drawn by the Earth's magnetic North and South polar regions.

Mountain goats have split hooves with sharp outer edges and a flexible rubbery sole, just like human climbing shoes. They give the goat a secure grip on even the most perilous foothold.

THE ROCKY MOUNTAINS: MOUNTAIN GOATS AND BIGHORN SHEEP

The mountain goat is the true master of the mountains. While others descend to warmer elevations or hibernate, the goats tough out the worst of the winter.

In the middle of winter, one hundred-mile-an-hour (161 kph) arctic winds blast the summit of Idaho's Pioneer Range. Yet the mountain goat calls these peaks home at twelve thousand feet (3,658 m). Here they feed on the tips of the highest growing trees, themselves at the limit of their range. These trees, mostly different kinds of fir and spruce, are survivors, like the goats, but the mountain conditions are so tough that they become stunted and twisted, a phenomenon known as Krumholtz formation.

In the summer, the mountain goats emerge from the misty summits and begin a perilous journey from the peaks to the valleys below. Having spent the winter eating twigs and lichens, they are driven by a need for vital mineral salt.

The nanny goats do a strange, prancing dance down the mountain. It helps shed her winter coat, and the younger goats, the kids, learn to mimic this. Their destination is the middle fork of the Flathead River in the Rocky Mountains. The steep cliffs here are rich in sodium, potassium, and calcium, vital minerals for the goats. So many goats congregate at this annual banquet that the cliff is covered with them. The goats travel down to the lick every few days, but return to the high peaks in between.

With the snow gone, they can climb even higher and reach the most impossible of places. And while others might struggle for a foothold, the goats are superbly adapted for life on these steep crumbling slopes and are natural rock climbers.

In the mountains, even in summer, things can change in an instant. Heavy rain in the high peaks can swell the river into a raging torrent and the goats have to find a way to cross to get to the salt they crave. The bigger goats can leap over, but for the smaller ones, it's daunting, and the prospect of getting swept away is very real.

As the summer days begin to shorten, it's a cue for another group of mountain heavyweights to limber up for a battle. The bighorn sheep can be found across the mountain ranges from Canada to Mexico. Their huge curved horns weigh up to thirty pounds (14 kg) and when the mating season arrives in the fall, the rams, charged with testosterone, fight to find a champion who will claim a group of females.

The males rear up on their hind legs and launch themselves at one another, charging at twenty miles an hour (32 kph). The clash of their horns can be heard echoing through the mountains. They will repeat the confrontation again and again, sometimes for hours, until one ram submits and walks away. Luckily their bony skulls usually prevent serious injury.

The lambs are born in the spring, on high, secluded ledges to protect them from bighorn predators such as wolves, coyotes, and mountain lions (cougars). The lambs can walk soon after birth and will rejoin the herds with their mothers when they are a week old.

CAVE OF THE CRYSTALS

In 2000 miners excavating a new tunnel uncovered a cave deep below the Naica peak in northern Mexico.

They couldn't believe what they saw in their torch beams; a chamber, filled with giant crystals—some over thirty feet (9 m) long. It became known as cueva de los cristales, or the cave of the crystals.

Scientists puzzled over how the crystals could have grown on such a giant scale. The answer lay deep in the earth, over a mile below the cave. The cave lies one thousand feet (305 m) beneath the earth's surface, and beneath the water table. A volcanic magma chamber heated the water in the cave, which was saturated with minerals. For over half a million years, the cave had remained filled with water at a stable 122°F (50°C) and this allowed the selenite crystals to form from the minerals, and to grow to such vast sizes. The geological forces that created these crystals are the same as those that create volcanoes, and that built the mountainous spine of North America.

The cave was only revealed when the water was pumped out as part of the mining operation—the mines in Naica produce silver, lead, and zinc—and pumps keep it clear. If the pumping were to be stopped, the cave would once again flood.

These are the biggest crystals in the world, the largest is over thirty-six feet (11 m) long, thirteen feet (4 m) in diameter, and weighs fifty-five tons (50,000 kg). But sadly, only a small number of people ever see them. The conditions in which the crystals exist have to be preserved, and the cave can only be entered with extreme caution. With temperatures of up to 136°F (58°C) and 90 to 99 percent humidity, you can only stay, even with special clothing and a breathing apparatus, for a matter of minutes.

When we obtained permission to shoot in the cave, we were allowed a maximum of two hours a day in there. To manage this, the crew went into the cave in relays, first to set up lights and equipment, and then to film.

To enter the cave, you must wear an ice vest, with ice-packs sewn into pockets across the chest and back. On top goes another vest to insulate the ice against the heat. A bright orange caving suit goes over the top, so that you can be easily spotted, with gloves and boots, a helmet with a headlamp, and a respirator mask blowing ice-cooled air.

As soon as you step inside the cave, the sweat pours off you, your heartbeat increases, and you feel exhausted. Heatstroke is a real possibility. But the physical demands of getting the footage were well worth the effort—to visit the cave of the crystals is an unforgettable experience—and one that will soon not be possible at all. The crystals deteriorate in air, so they are being recorded by scientists and in the near future, the cave will be resealed and allowed to flood again. We may have been the last team to document its wonders.

YELLOWSTONE

The Rockies of northern Wyoming are home to America's most famous supervolcano.

Mostly we think of volcanoes as cone-shapes, narrowing toward the top. So it can be hard to imagine that the huge, mostly forested, area of Yellowstone National Park is sitting inside the crater of a volcano that is 30 miles (48 km) across. Not only that, but the volcano is active—and though it has been six hundred thousand years since it last erupted, a vast magma chamber is bubbling away beneath the surface.

Yellowstone is at a high altitude, its highest point being over eleven thousand feet (3,353 m), and molten rock and lava erupt in thousands of mini earthquakes every year and fuel the ten thousand thermal features of the park, which include over half of the active geysers in the world. As well as between three hundred and five hundred geysers (hot springs that periodically throw water into the air), there are fumaroles, which eject steam; mudpots, which send showers of hot mud into the air; and steam vents through which steam hisses from underground, all of them heated by the underground thermal activity.

When winter is at its hardest for many North American animals, Yellowstone offers a refuge.

The geothermal action here makes it the warmest part of the caldera, the boiling steam keeps the geyser meadows largely free of snow, and there is a section of the Yellowstone River that doesn't freeze over. But even here, it can be so cold in winter that water exploding from geysers at over 200°F (93°C) freezes instantly into ice crystals, which rain from the sky.

Yellowstone National Park contains the world's
tallest active geyser, Steamboat Geyser, as
well as Old Faithful, which is the world's most
predictable geyser, erupting every 91 minutes.

Yellowstone was the
first National Park to
be established in North
America, back in 1872.
It's a designated World
Heritage Site of 3,472
square miles (8,992 sq km).

Many animals, from otters to ducks to bison, remain here to survive the winter. Among the sturdiest is the dipper, a small bird that survives by diving into winter ice holes in rivers and mountain streams that haven't completely iced over.

Taking a dip beneath the ice may sound cold, but the water is fifty degrees warmer than the mountain air. And the dippers are insulated by thick down and over six thousand soft feathers, coated in waterproof oil.

GRAND TETON MOUNTAINS, WYOMING: CALLIOPE HUMMINGBIRDS

While winter brings most animals down to the valleys and meadows, in summer, there are those that migrate up the mountains. Among them is the calliope hummingbird. This tiny bird forages for flowers in alpine meadows, feasting on nectar, and as the summer progresses, it will migrate up the mountain slopes. That's because the closer to the summit,

the longer the winter conditions last. So for every 100 feet (30 m) of elevation, flowering is delayed by a whole day.

In the Grand Teton Mountains, which is part of the Rocky Mountain chain in Wyoming, cow parsnip at the summit flowers a whole month after the same flowers at the mountain base, 3,300 feet (1,006 m) lower. And the hummingbirds follow this schedule of flowering, climbing higher up the mountain every few days. In the short mountain summer, time is of the essence, and competition for resources can get fierce. Weighing only an ounce (28 g), the calliope hummingbird is the smallest North American bird and its annual migration along the Rockies is the longest per gram of flesh of any warm-blooded creature.

Calliopes may be tiny, but they are feisty and determined. They will attack intruders that cross onto their "patch," even if they are much larger. And their love dances are impressive. When a female comes along during the mating season, the male will bring out his best moves to impress her, opening

his purple throat feathers during the dances before her.

No one really knows why they do this dance, but it may be that this display looks like a flower and is attractive to the female.

COSTA RICA: RESPLENDENT QUETZALS

Not all the mountains of America are covered with snow. In Costa Rica, in the far south of the Pacific-American chain, there are tropical peaks. Here the mountain-dwelling trees of the cloud forests are battered by the winds and rain, and only have the energy to become miniature versions of their low-altitude cousins.

These mountains are home to one very special bird. Its feathers were used to decorate the headdresses of local chieftains, and many describe it as the most beautiful bird in the world; the resplendent quetzal, with its red chest and gleaming, iridescent green-gold wing, back chest, and head feathers.

The lives of these beautiful birds are dictated by the mountains and the influence they have on the local weather. As the seasons change, moisture-laden clouds climb up the mountainsides. When the clouds break, torrential rains trigger the fruiting of the sweet Lauraceae (laurel) avocado, and the quetzal must be ready. The avocados provide the quetzals with the fatty goodness they need to give them the energy to breed, but to obtain them, the quetzals must make lonely solo migrations, up to 3,280 feet (1,000 m) into the cloud forest. In return for the bounty, the bird will swallow the avocado seeds and disperse them through the forest.

The mountain weather causes a seasonal abundance, and the clever quetzal has learned to make the most of it.

Quetzal means
"precious" in the
Mayan language.

Yosemite National Park covers more than 760,000 acres and is well known for its spectacular granite cliffs. El Capitan (on the left) rises about 3,000 feet (900 m) from base to summit. Bridalveil Falls (on the right) is 617 feet (188 m) and flows year-round.

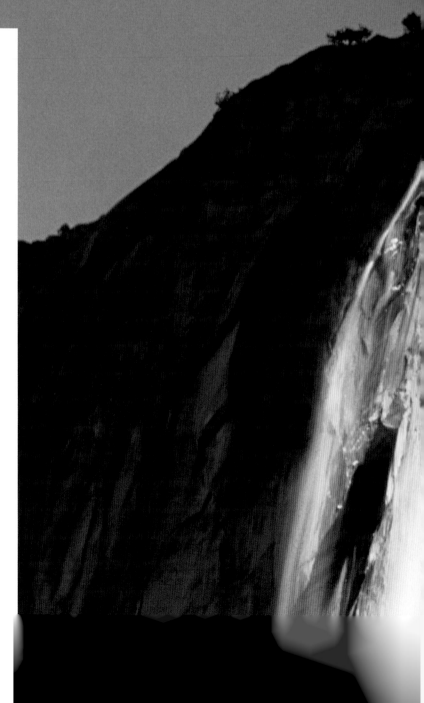

Horsetail Falls

The melting winter snow causes a miraculous phenomenon that indicates spring in Yosemite Park, situated on the western slopes of the Californian Sierra Madre mountains.

Yosemite Valley is in the Yosemite National Park, and is known for its spectacular granite cliffs and rock formations, which include the towering faces of Cathedral Spires and Half Dome. It also includes the 350-story rock walls of El Capitan, a granite monolith three thousand feet (914 m) high. These walls are a famous challenge for rock climbers and, for a brief time each February, they become the canvass for one of the most beautiful mountain spectacles in North America.

As the melted water pours down the slopes of El Capitan, it cascades for one thousand feet (305 m) over Horsetail Falls. And for a few days each spring, the setting sun is at the correct angle to light up the falls, transforming the water into golden flames.

The falls only light up for fifteen minutes every evening, before fading away with the setting sun. And once the snows of winter have melted by April, the falls will cease to tumble.

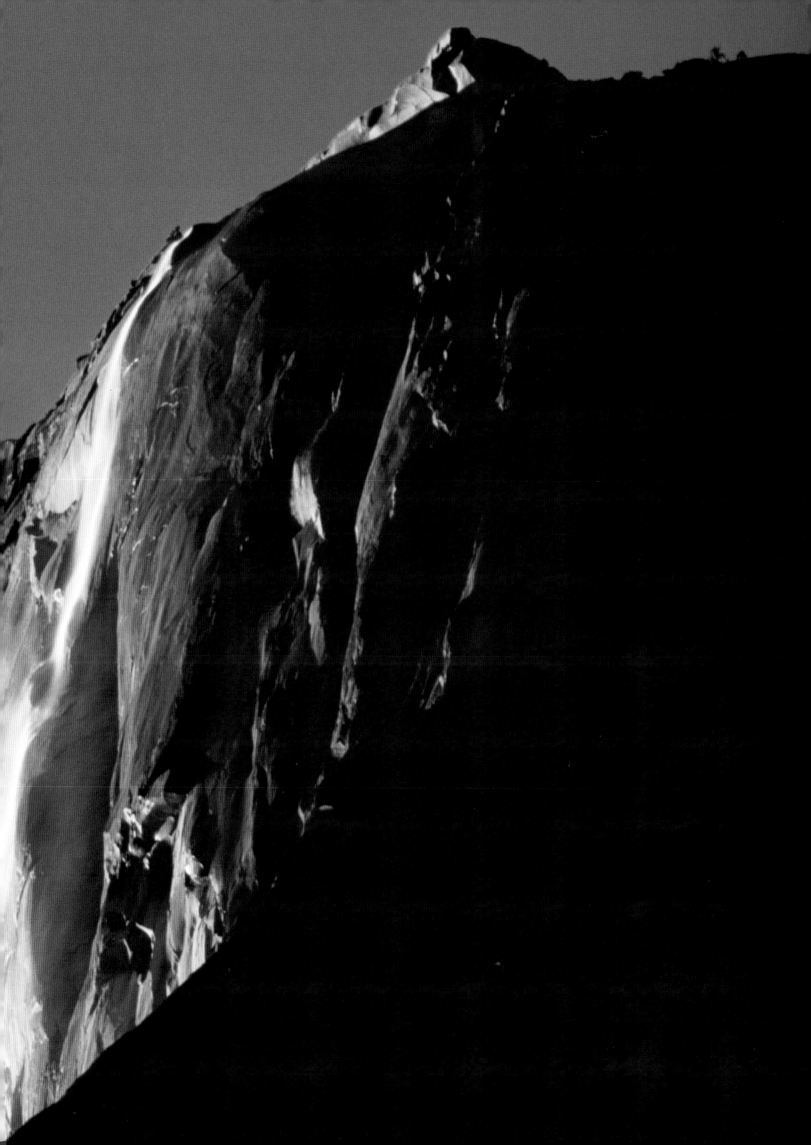

Wolverines

The wolverine is one of North America's most formidable animal mountaineers.

The largest member of the weasel family, the wolverine is stocky and muscular and looks like a small bear. It is perfectly equipped to live in snowy and mountainous regions with large five-toed paws that make it easy to move through deep snow and a thick, dark, oily fur that is resistant to frost.

Wolverines are solitary animals that will roam over a territory of five hundred square miles (1295 sq km), traveling as much as fifteen miles (24 km) in a day, patrolling the slopes in search of victims of avalanches or dead carrion, and following routes that take them across the toughest terrain.

They have been spotted crossing high altitude passes at thirteen thousand feet (3,962 m). And they eat anything they can find—even if it's frozen solid. They have a powerful sense of smell that can find a carcass buried twenty feet (6.1 m) beneath the snow, powerful jaws, and a special upper molar tooth in the back of the mouth, rotated ninety degrees toward the inside of the mouth, which allows them to tear off meat from prey that has been frozen.

Amazingly strong for their size, wolverines are predators and scavengers. They have been known to steal food from other predators, and their voracious eating style has given them the nickname gluttons, though this habit of gobbling is simply a response to the scarcity of food in their inhospitable habitat.

CHAPTER FIVE

RAGING
RAPIDS

Rivers are enormously important to the natural life of North America. Productive, powerful, and often astonishingly beautiful, these channels of energy, communication, and sustenance, provide habitats for thousands of species of plants and animals.

The power of water has always drawn us to it—there is no other element with which we share such an affinity, perhaps because it is the giver of life for us, too, and the freshwater channels of our planet are vital to us.

All rivers, no matter how large or small, how wide or narrow, start at a high point inland and flow to a body of water—either the sea or a lake. A river's source might be a mountain, or simply higher ground, where surface water from a spring, a lake, or melting snow begins to flow downward.

As it flows, it will usually link up with other rivers or streams and grow bigger, sometimes into a vast river that stretches for thousands of miles. These rivers have watersheds—drainage areas—stretching across vast swathes of North America.

Rivers are the arteries of life. They are used like roads for transport; they create fertile plains; they carry nutrients, gases, and organisms that enrich and feed the soil and the creatures in and around the river; and, of course, they provide life-giving water.

Rivers also help to shape the earth, both carving the land and building it up. As they flow they cut into the landscape, changing its shape and shifting soil and rocks from one place to another, so that new land formations are created.

The Mississippi River, when combined with its tributary the Missouri, is the fourth longest in the world, after the Nile in Africa, the Amazon in South America, and the Yangtze in China.

Mayflies will only hatch in clean water, so
when they hatch in large numbers, it's a sign
that the fish in that area will be healthy.

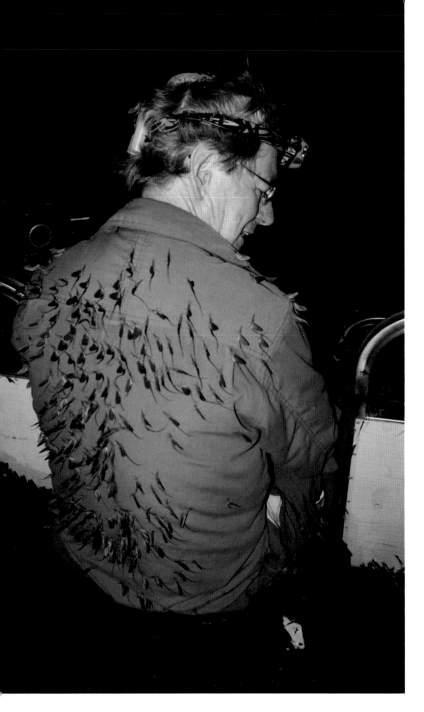

THE MISSISSIPPI: MAYFLIES

Of the many hundreds of rivers throughout North America, none is better known, more powerful, or more vital than the great Mississippi. This extraordinary river, the longest in North America, begins its journey at Lake Itaska, a small glacial lake in Clearwater County, Minnesota. Lake Itaska is fed by several tributaries, one of which is the true source of the river. From the outflow of Lake Itasca, the Mississippi, which starts at just twenty to thirty feet (6 to 9 m) wide, flows for approximately 2,320 miles (3,734 km) down to the Mississippi River Delta at the Gulf of Mexico. This journey takes the river three months as it flows through the ten US states of Louisiana, Mississippi, Arkansas, Tennessee, Kentucky, Missouri, Illinois, Iowa, Wisconsin, and Minnesota. At its widest, at Lake

Winnibigoshish, near Bena, Minnesota, it is more than seven miles (11 km) wide, and with its many tributaries, its watershed covers 1.8 million square miles (4.7 million sq km), draining thirty-two states—41 percent of the United States—and two Canadian provinces, making it the third largest drainage basin in the world.

Thousands of species of fish, birds, mammals, reptiles, amphibians, and insects make river ecosystems their home, and the amazing system of waterways that is the Mississippi supports a phenomenal array of life, including 241 species of fish. And 60 percent of all North American birds (326 species) use the Mississippi River Basin as their migratory flyway. Among them are huge numbers of tree swallows, a native North American species, which gather along the banks of the river each evening to roost. As one enormous flock after another swoops in, another great emergence of life is happening in the river.

Billions of mayflies hatch every year on the Mississippi. Each one lives for only a day, but there are so many that they provide food for an enormous range of animals in and around the river.

To capture this momentous event was surprisingly difficult. First, hatching isn't always predictable, and second, since they hatch at night, recording the hatching is tricky.

Our camera team took to the water on a pontoon, with four different cameras, including high-speed and infrared, and for four weeks they patrolled the river, waiting for the hatching to begin.

Once they began to hatch, the mayflies were everywhere—clogging up the camera lenses, getting inside clothing, and so thick in the air that the team needed masks to avoid swallowing them.

For two hours every night, like clockwork, the hatching went on, with the new hatchlings taking to the air as the females that had hatched the night before danced back onto the river to lay their eggs, their last act before dying. These eggs will sink into the river and develop into naiads, the immature stage of the mayfly, which will live in the water for a year before emerging.

And as the mayflies emerged, so did those waiting to feed on them, a springtime boom of birds, including blackbirds, tits, gulls, and grackles, frogs and fish leaping from the water, and raccoons and muskrats along the banks.

THE SWAMPLANDS: ALLIGATOR GARS, ALLIGATORS, CROCODILES, AND MANATEES

It's not just the river itself that is filled with life. The Atchafalaya Swamp in southern Louisiana is a distributary of the Mississippi—an enormous wetland basin to the west of the river created by flooding, when the river's banks simply can't contain the vast amount of water pouring down its channels.

The Atchafalaya, a large part of which is a National Wildlife Refuge, is the largest swamp in the United States, filled with bayous—marshy lakes or wetlands and brackish areas. And in this rich, shallow swampland that measures 20 miles by 150 miles (32 km by 241 km) live a myriad of creatures.

It is situated at the mouth of North America's most important flyway and supports half of the continent's migratory waterfowl and many land birds, too, more than three hundred bird species in all. There are also around one hundred species of fish, crawfish, shrimp, and crabs, all of which provide food for birds and for huge numbers of reptiles and mammals.

Among the more unusual of the swamp's inhabitants is the alligator gar—North America's largest exclusively freshwater fish. This huge monster of a fish is prehistoric; it has existed for millions of years, roaming the rivers, swamps, and bayous of the southeast United States and is considered to be a living dinosaur.

There are seven members of the gar fish family, and the alligator gar is the biggest and scariest. Named because of their alligator-like snout and double row of razor-sharp teeth, these fish regularly reach lengths of eight to ten feet (2.4 to 3 m) and can weigh three to four hundred pounds (136 to 181 kg).

Alligator gar survive in the brackish swamp waters because they come up to the surface and gulp air. They have been accused of attacks on humans, but no attack has ever been proven. It may be that the fish's fearsome reputation is undeserved and that it has been blamed for attacks that were actually carried out by their neighbors in the swamp, the alligators.

There are more than a million alligators in the Louisiana swamplands and the same number in Florida, where the

Alligator gar are the largest freshwater fish in North America. Growing to more than 300 pounds, their diamond-shaped scales are interlocking (or ganoid) to form a nearly impenetrable armor.

Everglades is a vast area of wetlands, sawgrass marshes, and forests, fed by the Crystal, Silver, and Rainbow Rivers. It is a unique ecosystem and is a National Park and World Heritage Site that supports a huge range of animal and plant species.

Alligators, despite their fierce reputation and fearsome appearance, are reasonably easygoing creatures. We filmed them in the crystal clear waters of the Silver River and apart from the occasional curious gator, they swam past—or sometimes over—us, without taking much notice. Crocodiles, which share the Everglades with them but don't venture as far north as the Silver River, are snappier and more aggressive. And unlike the crocodile, which needs warmth to survive, the alligator can withstand dramatic drops in temperature and even remain locked in ice for up to three

Manatees

Manatees can grow up to thirteen feet (4 m) long, weigh fifteen hundred to eighteen hundred pounds (680 to 816 kg) and live up to sixty years. They have grayish-brown thick, wrinkled skin and propel themselves along with flippers and a large, flat tail. They evolved over millions of years from land mammals, and their closest living relatives are the elephant and the hyrax. Manatees breathe through their nostrils, but they have large lungs, two-thirds the length of their bodies, so they can remain underwater for up to twenty minutes at a time.

Most manatees spend half their day sleeping in the water and the other half grazing on underwater plants. They are generally solitary creatures, unless mating, caring for their young, or sheltering in warm springs. A female will give birth about once every three years to a single calf, which will stay with her for twelve to eighteen months.

Manatees communicate with one another by using a wide range of sounds underwater to indicate stress, fear, or excitement and are believed to have an intelligence level similar to that of dolphins. Their number has dropped dramatically in recent years, and they are now a protected species. Many of the manatees in Florida bear the scars of boat propellers.

Manatees are gentle and slow-moving animals with few natural predators. Since manatees cannot survive very long in water below 68 degrees Fahrenheit in winter they congregate around warm water springs.

weeks, with just a small breathing hole. All a bystander will see is the tip of its snout poking through the ice and it will slow its body functions to virtually shut down.

When the alligators bellow, you can hear it echo across the swamplands, as one begins and others take up the call until dozens of them are doing it. Amusingly, anything that sounds like another alligator can set them off, from a deep bass note in the music of a passing car, to the space shuttle, which set them all off for a radius of fifty miles every time it launched. Only the males bellow, giving out a deep throaty rumble, and although it can happen at any time of year, it's more common during the mating season.

While we were filming alligators, several manatees arrived. Large, slow-moving marine mammals, they are sometimes known as sea cows. Such a large family of these harmless and good-natured creatures hadn't been seen in the Silver River for many years. They are generally tropical animals that live most of the year around the southern Florida coast, in the balmy waters of the Caribbean. But they struggle to survive if the water temperature drops below 65°F (18°C), and because they can live in both fresh and salt water, in the winter months, many travel north to Florida's waterways, especially the warm springs.

Manatees are herbivorous and live on underwater plants.

There are very few plants in the springs. They can manage without food for a couple of weeks, but eventually hunger will drive them back to the sea.

Florida is the northern limit of where both the manatees and the crocodiles can survive year-round. During the first winter in which we filmed, it was unexpectedly cold and sadly the Everglades lost 40 percent of its crocodiles and 30 percent of its manatees.

YELLOWSTONE: OTTERS AND GOLDENEYE DUCKS

The Yellowstone River is a tributary of the Missouri, which runs, for a good deal of its 692 miles (1,114 km), through the Yellowstone National Park.

In the winter, many North American rivers freeze over. But in Yellowstone, because of the underground heat, stretches of the river stay open, providing a much-needed source of food for otters. The North American river otter, a member of the weasel family, is just as happy on dry ground as in the water, and builds a burrow next to the water with entrances on land as well as directly into the water. They eat fish and that means they need access to water, where the fish are, no matter what the time of year. So when stretches of the river are iced up, the otters will head for those places where

The Great Lakes hold 22 percent
of the world's freshwater.

The otter's coat is extremely dens. With 156,000 hairs per square inch, it is specifically designed to keep out the cold.

the water is still accessible.

Whiskers on the otters' muzzles help them sense small fish hidden among the stones on the bottom, and the otters will work together to catch them.

Winter in Yellowstone is incredibly beautiful, but it's a cruel time, and animals have to work hard to survive—and to watch out for predators. We filmed a group of goldeneye ducks escaping the attentions of a stalking bobcat, while diving to feed on the river bottom. The ducks were close to the head of one of the Yellowstone River's many waterfalls, and as they bobbed between the ice floes that had been washed downstream, one little duck was caught in the flow and swept over the edge. Down it went—it was a long drop—and it reappeared in the pool at the bottom and was battered against the icy bank by the swirling torrent. Too waterlogged to fly, it looked as though the duck wouldn't make it until, with a

stroke of luck, it was swept onto the bank.

Frozen lakes and rivers can be as cruel as deserts, yet somehow life endures with the promise of spring and the spectacular change it brings—the thawing of the ice and snow and the release of the full potential of fresh water.

PLATTE RIVER, NEBRASKA: SANDHILL CRANES

As longer days warm the north and the snow and ice start to retreat, Sandhill cranes arrive in Nebraska, on this ninety-mile (145 km) stretch of the Platte River, halfway through their journey from Mexico to their breeding grounds in the Northwest Territories of Canada and as far as Siberia.

As the days pass, more and more cranes arrive, creating a truly spectacular scene. Half a million birds, an astonishing 80 percent of the world's population, gather here. Their

journey takes the cranes several weeks, and by the time they reach the Platte, most of them have lost a fifth of their bodyweight. They need to feed, rest, and replenish for a few weeks before they go on.

Cranes congregate at this spot because the river's wetlands provide an abundance of the food they need; there are insects, fish, frogs, and corn from the neighboring fields. Farmers don't mind the cranes since they don't damage the crops.

They bathe, preen, feed, and make a huge volume of noise. Their unique trumpeting call is thought to be the oldest sound in North America. Fossil evidence has shown that sandhill cranes have been coming to this same spot for about 10 million years. So their sound is that of an extinct age.

They're large birds that can weigh up to fourteen pounds (6.4 kg) and have a wingspan of five to six feet (1.5 to 1.8 m).

They are also entertaining to watch, coming in to land in a slightly comical way, with their legs straight out in front.

We filmed the cranes gathering on the Platte two years running. They're easily spooked, and once frightened, they won't come back to the same spot, so we built a hide on the riverbank (see the top photograph on the opposite page) where our dedicated cameraman slept, so that he could film the birds first thing in the morning.

The first year, the El Niño year, once again, the weather did not follow its usual pattern. There was a late snowstorm and the cranes route north was blocked. They had no choice but to wait it out, bitterly cold and buffeted by the winds, until the weather finally cleared and, en masse, they were able to take off for the rest of their journey. The second year the weather was fine and the cranes were able to take off on time.

CAHABA RIVER, ALABAMA: REDEYE BASS AND MUSSELS

In the warmer days of spring, rivers and streams buzz with an explosion of new life. And on a beautiful stretch of the longest river in Alabama, the Cahaba, there's a fascinating little drama being enacted under the water's surface.

Redeye bass may be small—they are around six inches (15 cm) long—but they are voracious predators that will intimidate and bully each other—and any other creature unfortunate enough to cross their path. But this aggression is perfect for the freshwater mussels that use it to solve a problem.

If the mussels release their eggs, they'll just go downstream and most will end up in the sea and be lost. They need a courier to take their eggs to new locations where mussels can grow and thrive, and the mobile bass is the perfect candidate. So the mussels produce a lure that looks just like a flapping fish. This is irresistible to a hungry bass, which

pounces, hoping for an easy meal. But it's a trick—the lure hides the mussel's eggs and as the fish bites, they are released into its mouth.

The bass is not happy. It heads away, unknowingly taking the eggs with it, which settle into its gills. Two weeks later, the baby mussels are ready. Still tinier than a grain of sand, they release from the fish's gills and drop to the bottom of the river, ready to colonize a new area.

Evolutionary biologist Stephen Jay Gould said that one of his favorite examples of evolution in action was the behavior of these mussels. By fooling the bass, and hitching a ride to new locations, tucked safely into the bass's nurturing gills, they are following the need all living beings have, to perpetuate their species.

Mollusks are vital to the health of river systems; their ability to filter water makes them natural purifiers, so the mussels' use of the bass as a means of transport has far wider implications than simply the survival of a species. The farther the mussels travel, the better it will be for our waterways.

RAPIDS OF THE DROWNED: PELICANS

The Slave River runs from Lake Athabaska, in northeastern Alberta, Canada, to the Great Slave Lake, which is in the Northwest Territories, inside the Arctic Circle.

The Slave River's name is thought to come from the Slavey group of First Nations people, and has nothing to do with slavery. And on its 269-mile (433 km) route, its steady flow is broken only once, by a series of dramatic rapids that provide some of the best whitewater kayaking in the world.

Rapids form when rivers meet rock, and on the Slave River there are four sets of rapids: Pelican, Rapids of the Drowned, Mountain Portage, and Cassette. The rapids range from relatively easy kayaking to the unrunnable Rapids of the Drowned. Three-quarters of a mile wide and lethal, these rapids provide a natural fish trap that attracts huge numbers of the American white pelican, which nest on islands in the river.

This is the most northerly pelican colony in the world, and they gather here in summer to breed and feed on fish from the river. While some pelicans dive for fish, these catch their food by swimming on the surface of the water. They are social birds that fish by working together in the pockets of calmer water behind the main rapids, beating their wings on the surface of the water to drive the fish into the shallows where they can scoop them up.

Pelicans are large birds with huge beaks and the famous throat pouch. These elastic pouches are used to catch fish. They scoop up the fish, tip their beaks to drain out the water—some pouches can hold up to three gallons (117 l)—and then swallow the fish. Contrary to belief, they don't use their pouches to store fish.

American white pelicans fly together, often in a V-shaped formation. They migrate to the Slave River from

Pelicans have a complex communal courtship. Males will chase a single female while pointing, gaping, and thrusting their bills at each other.

the southern states and Mexico and have their young on islands where they are protected from predators. Any kind of human interference will put pelicans off a nesting site permanently, so it's vital that they are not disturbed.

Pelican parents build shallow nests on the ground and both parents take turns incubating the eggs—usually two or three—which take about a month to hatch. The young feed by taking fish from their parent's throats and often only the strongest chick survives because the weaker ones can't compete for food. The chicks fledge after about ten weeks.

Pelicans are full of character and very sociable; they will form lines to fish together, but then squabble over their catch. We filmed them flying above the falls, and they were extremely relaxed flying alongside us. In the golden light of the Arctic sunrise, it was a magnificent sight.

GREAT SALT LAKE: BRINE FLIES

The Great Salt Lake in the US state of Utah is filled with minerals, deposited there by the three major rivers—the Bear, the Weber, and the Jordan—that flow into it. These rivers have absorbed the minerals from the rocks they flow over on their path down from the Uinta mountain range to the lake.

Every year, these rivers bring 2.2 million tons of salty deposits down to the lake, making it seven times saltier than the sea. The lake is surrounded by mountains and has no outlet, and as it is a desert region and is shallow, much of the water evaporates, leaving mineral salt deposits around the edges. So although it covers an area of roughly 1,700 square

miles (4,430 sq km), it can shrink to as little as 950 square miles (2,460 sq km).

The result is a dry, salty area that can stretch for many miles, that is inhospitable and desolate. How can anything possibly survive here? And yet it does. This is the perfect home for the brine fly, a small fly that thrives in salty conditions and that, in turn, attracts many shorebirds and waterfowl, all of which come to feed on it.

Around the Great Salt Lake, brine flies hatch in their billions. Their concentration can reach 370 million per mile of shoreline, and for the birds that feed on them, it's a welcome bonanza—so welcome that some of them don't

With gaping beaks, gulls feast on the brine fly swarm.

know when to stop. The California gulls gorge themselves on brine flies to the point where they are too fat to fly and can only waddle around, waiting for the excess to wear off! It was a comical sight—gulls running at full speed, beaks open to scoop in flies, as though Christmas had come early.

The Great Salt Lake is the remnant of a prehistoric lake that was more than ten times bigger, extending for twenty thousand square miles (51,800 sq km). Lake Bonneville covered much of western Utah and parts of Idaho and Nevada during the Great Ice Age, which lasted between thirty-two thousand and fourteen thousand years ago. About seventeen thousand years ago, a massive outlet appeared at the northern end of the lake, and a huge flood of 159 gallons (602 l) a second flowed out, leaving the Great Salt Lake, Utah Lake, Sevier Lake, and Rush Lake as remnants.

SOCKEYE SALMON, BROWN BEARS, AND BALD EAGLES

Every year sockeye salmon invade the Fraser River, the longest river in British Columbia. Rising at Fraser Pass in the Rocky Mountains, the river flows for 854 miles (1,374 km) into the Strait of Georgia at Vancouver. It's the largest salmon-producing river in the world. In 2010, there was the biggest run of salmon in living memory; around 34 million fish entered the river.

As the salmon battle upstream to their spawning grounds, they're on the last leg of a two-and-a-half-thousand-mile (4,023 km) journey from the Pacific Ocean back to their Canadian spawning grounds. Salmon begin their lives in freshwater, usually spending their first two or three years in a lake, and then travel to the open ocean, where they feed and grow for the next one to four years, before beginning the incredible journey back to where they were hatched.

Salmon from the rivers of North America provide a vital food source for all kinds of animals, including one very ingenious group of brown bears on Kodiak Island, off the coast of Alaska. Kodiak is the second largest island in the United States, after Hawaii, and it's home to some of the largest bears in the world. But despite their size, these bears can be amazingly graceful swimmers.

Not many bears choose to catch their salmon in a deep lake, but a handful do, and we were able to film, for the first time ever, exactly how they do it. Bears had been spotted disappearing under the water in Karluk Lake and reappearing

The sockeye is among the smallest of the seven Pacific salmon species, but their succulent, bright-orange meat is prized above all others.

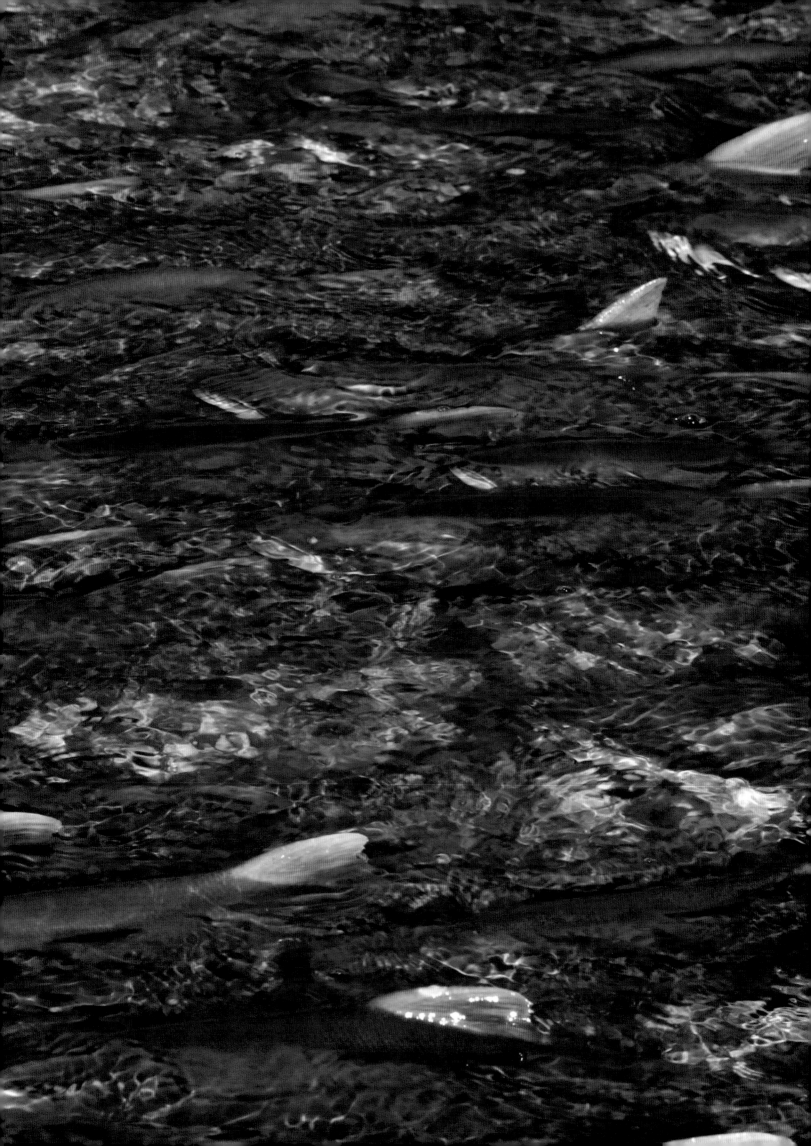

with salmon, but no one knew what happened next. Were they diving? And if so, how were they getting fish off the bottom? It took the skill of a cameraman with an inventive streak to come up with a way for us to film what the bears were up to underwater. We couldn't send a diver down there; he or she would have had to wait underwater for a bear to arrive, which might have taken hours or days, and it might also have been very dangerous. So our cameraman, Nick Guy, came up with a remote-control floating camera in a submarine-shaped casing that was capable of going underwater.

Nick and assistant producer Alicia Decina spent six weeks at the lake, perfecting the sub, getting to know the bears' habits, and capturing some unique footage of the bears diving. We had wondered whether they went down feet first, but the sub confirmed that they dived head first to depths of up to twenty feet (6 m) and picked up fish with their paws, before returning, back legs tucked underneath, to the surface.

All the bears were females and had refined diving skills that are rare in bears. They were driven to learn these new skills in order to feed their cubs. Being able to go down into the lake helps both mother and cub to fatten up before hibernation.

Over on the Chilkat River, in the mountains of mainland Alaska, the salmon provide nourishment for a very different animal. The Chilkat has the last salmon run in southeast Alaska, because its waters remain warm and ice-free throughout the year, creating a unique environment. During the months from October to February, more than thirty-five hundred bald eagles will congregate there—the largest bald eagle gathering in the world—for a late salmon run. As the eagles descend on the river, competition for the salmon is intense, and fights break out. These eagles weigh about thirteen pounds (6 kg), have a wingspan of seven feet (2.1 m), and have a razor-sharp beak and talons to match, so fights can be ferocious and the winner of the prized salmon will carry it off to the trees on the river bank—providing they can carry it. A bald eagle can manage to carry five pounds (2.3 kg), so she will eat what she can of a bigger fish until flying with it is possible.

This gathering of the bald eagles is a big annual event—hundreds of people come to watch and photograph them every year. Our camera team worked from a hide on the gravel bars at the side of the river, using super slow-motion to obtain unique footage of these dramatic and fast-moving birds.

The Hay River and Alexandra Falls

Alexandra Falls sits on the Hay River in the Northwest Territories of Canada. This is a highly unusual river because it flows south to north—most rivers flow north to south. In winter, the Hay is iced over, but because of the direction of flow, the ice on the river doesn't melt slowly when spring arrives. Instead, it is hit by a pulse of warm water that flows up from the south and breaks the ice into huge blocks. And when that happens, the explosion of ice thundering over the waterfall is an amazing sight.

This annual spring melt can never be accurately predicted—scientists know it's coming, but can't pinpoint exactly when, and even the seasoned townspeople who live down river in the town of Hay River, seldom get it dead right. So our team arrived on the banks of the waterfall a few weeks before the melt was due, and joined the scientists and spectators to wait it out.

One morning, five weeks later, the dull roar of the waterfall became a thunderous crashing, as the warm current surged toward it and enormous blocks of ice, weighing hundreds of tons, were hurled over the fall's 100-foot (30 m) drop. It was an extraordinary sight, a dramatic event that began with a crack in the ice and was over in twenty minutes.

CHAPTER SIX

OUTLAWS AND SKELETONS

The deserts of North America lie down the western side of the United States and across the border into Mexico. Deserts are often seen as barren wastelands, but they are biologically rich habitats with many animals and plants that have adapted to the harsh conditions. And North America's deserts are the richest of any in the world, because they lie in the path of violent rainstorms.

If an area receives an average of less than ten inches (25 cm) of rain each year, scientists classify it as a desert. A desert is not defined by heat but is a place where more water is lost through evaporation than is gained through precipitation, so deserts can also be cold; by this definition, the Arctic and Antarctic are desert regions.

True deserts cover about 14 percent of the world's land area, or about 8,000,000 square miles (20,719,905 sq km). Another 15 percent of the Earth's land surface possesses some desertlike characteristics.

In North America, the proportion of desert in each country varies enormously. Almost a third of Mexico, 29 percent, is desert. Just over 5 percent of the United States is desert, and there are no deserts in the remainder of Central America or in Canada, so the proportion of desert in the whole of North America is small. Some areas called deserts are not, in fact, true deserts; in Canada, the Nk'Mip Desert is

actually shrub steppe and the "desert" near Carcross, Yukon, is an area of northern sand dunes.

There are four major North American deserts, three of which are linked. The Great BasinDesert lies across regions of Idaho, Nevada, Oregon, and Utah; the Sonoran Desert is in regions of Arizona and California, the Baja California Peninsula, and part of the state of Sonora in Mexico. The smaller Mojave Desert covers parts of California, Arizona, and Nevada, and bridges the Great Basin and the Sonoran Deserts. The Mojave contains the grimly titled Death Valley, where the lowest, driest, and hottest locations in North America are found. The largest North American desert, the Chihuahuan, lies mostly in Mexico, crossing into Arizona, New Mexico, and Texas.

These deserts lie in a large basin between the Rocky Mountains to the east, and the Sierra Nevada to the west. They are in the "rain shadow" of the mountains on either side; rain falls on the mountains and not in the lower-lying regions in between. Each summer, the North America monsoon arrives over the southwest United States and northwest Mexico, bringing thunderstorms that drench some desert areas, supplying over half their water for the year in just hours.

Although the Great Basin, Mojave, and Sonoran are connected, they are categorized as separate deserts

Global warming threatens to change the ecology of deserts. Higher temperatures may produce an increasing number of wildfires that alter desert landscapes by eliminating slow-growing trees and shrubs and replacing them with fast-growing grasses.

The deserts of Arizona can have as many as 600,000 lightning strikes a year.

Badlands, South Dakota, got its name because it is such difficult terrain to travel over. The Lakota Native Americans called this area *Makhosica*, which means "bad land," and French trappers called it *les mauvaises terries à traverser*, which means "the bad lands to cross."

The Monsoon

The monsoon known as the North American monsoon or the Mexican monsoon, falls over large areas of the southwest United States and northwest Mexico, turning a baked and parched June into a torrential July.

In the buildup to the monsoon, warm moist air from the Gulf of Mexico condenses and is lifted to form giant cumulus clouds—some twice as high as Mount Everest—and building electrical energy that explodes repeatedly as lightning. A single lightning bolt can generate a billion volts and reach temperatures of fifty thousand degrees, and the North American monsoon can generate hundreds of lightning bolts every year.

The violent rainstorms of the monsoon, known as downbursts, don't fall everywhere. They hit the ground in patches across the desert, so that while some places remain dry, in others, this may be the first rain that has fallen in several years.

As much as five inches (13 cm) of rain can fall in a few hours. The parched ground can't soak up this much water, and flash floods can race across the desert.

Antelope Canyon, formed by flash floods eroding the sandstone, is the most photographed slot canyon in America.

because they have different characteristics, vegetation, and animals. The Great Basin Desert is classified as cold due to its more northern latitude and higher elevations; most of it is at least three thousand feet (914 m) above sea level, and more commonly four thousand (1,219 m) to 6,500 feet (1,981 m). Precipitation here is more evenly distributed throughout the year than in the other three North American deserts, and in winter often falls as snow.

Though the storms can bring welcome respite, for most of the year water is desperately scarce. Desert plants that survive are those that need little moisture, and for many of the animals that make the deserts their home, life is a continual search for water.

DESERT ANIMALS

The North American deserts harbor an abundant variety of insects, reptiles, birds, and mammals. So how do they all survive? Most desert animals have evolved ways to solve the heat and water problems the desert environment creates. Many get water from secondary sources and have no need to drink. Lizards, snakes, and other reptiles get moisture from plant fluids or animals they have eaten, while desert birds also obtain most or all of their moisture from the insects and spiders that they eat. Rodents, including mice, rats, and squirrels, rabbits, and bats, are the most numerous mammals. Most are essentially nocturnal and remain underground during the heat of the day and, like the birds and reptiles, they obtain moisture from their food. Higher up in the food

In 1971 a federal law was passed banning
the capture or harm of mustangs roaming
on public land, after the United States
Congress called them "living symbols of the
pioneer spirit of the West."

chain, carnivores such as coyotes, bobcats, foxes, and skunks must find water sources, but many of these animals are able to travel substantial distances between waterholes, which smaller animals could not manage. Desert bighorn sheep, one of the larger desert mammals, don't need drinking water in winter when green vegetation is available. During the summer months, they only need to visit waterholes every few days.

GREAT BASIN DESERT: MUSTANGS AND PYGMY RABBITS

The Great Basin Desert covers an arid expanse of about 158,000 square miles (409,218 sq km) of Idaho, Nevada, Oregon, and Utah. This is sometimes called North America's biggest desert because the Colorado Plateau, in northeast Arizona, can be included in its definition. But while this region includes large barren areas and spectacular geological formations, it is not a true desert.

In contrast to the other three deserts, Great Basin vegetation is low and homogenous, often with a single dominant species of bush that continues for miles. Typical shrubs include sagebrush, shadscale, greasewood, blackbrush, and Mormon tea, and there are very few types of cactus. The animals of the Great Basin include bighorn sheep, the jackrabbit, the pocket mouse, pronghorn antelope, the sage thrasher, and the side-blotched lizard.

The Great Basin is also home to one of North America's most symbolic and familiar animals—the wild American mustang. These free-roaming horses are not truly wild. They are descended from domestic horses brought to North

America by the Spanish conquistadors over five hundred years ago and are classified as feral.

These were not the first horses in North America. Primitive horses roamed the continent in prehistoric times, but they died out at the end of the last ice age, due to the climactic change and to the arrival of hunters.

When the conquistadors arrived bringing horses back to America, beginning with Columbus in 1493, the Native Americans took to them, and quickly the horse became the major means of transport and an integral part of Native American culture. But as other means of transportation were developed, such as trains and cars, the horse became less necessary.

Only one hundred years ago, there were over two million free-roaming mustangs, but by the 1920s, five hundred a day were slaughtered for pet food, a practice that was only stopped in the 1950s.

Today there are around twenty-five thousand mustang horses that roam the deserts and plains and are protected by law. Over half the mustang herds are in Nevada, and there are others in Montana, Wyoming, Utah, California, New Mexico, and Oregon.

Small, fast, and sure-footed, mustangs today are descendants of a mix of breeds. An average of fourteen hands high (4.6 ft or 1.4 m), measured at the base of the neck, they can be black, brown, bay, or gray. In the wild, they live for fifteen to twenty years, though those in captivity can live ten years longer. Intelligent and high-spirited, they travel in herds, animal behavior that originally developed because they were safer and more able to spot predators while grouped together.

Mustangs' strong legs and hooves make them less prone to injury than many domestic horses and they also have enormous stamina; the herds can travel for over one thousand miles between desert springs.

A herd generally consists of a stallion and seven or eight mares, plus their foals. At the age of two, the young males, or colts, will be driven away by the stallion. Colts form all-male herds until they are mature and each manages to attract his own herd of mares.

Herds have their own territories and they have adapted to live in desert areas by developing a tolerance to a low-nutrition diet of juniper plants, sagebrush, and coarse grasses.

While summers in the Great Basin are blisteringly hot, the elevation means that snow in winter is common.

The world's smallest rabbit, the pygmy rabbit, is the size of a soda can. It survives without water by chewing sagebrush.

Summer or winter, water is scarce, but one of the valley's smallest inhabitants, the pygmy rabbit, has adapted to this.

The size of a soda can, it is the world's smallest rabbit. But despite its size, it is a resourceful survivor, living largely on sagebrush, which contains a tiny amount of water in each leaf. It takes a lot of chewing, but if the rabbit eats enough of the plant, it has no need to drink.

In winter the rabbits avoid sinking deep into the snow by making trails to get from one clump of sagebrush to another. It also helps them to avoid the rabbits' chief predator, the weasel. Other predators include hawks, owls, coyotes, red foxes, and badgers and with so many animals after them, 88 percent of these tiny rabbits die from predation. The majority don't make

Haboobs

Haboobs—the name means strong wind in Arabic—are enormous dust storms that sometimes follow the desert monsoon or other big thunderstorms. As the storm collapses, energy is forced from its center, in the form of a great wind. This wind picks up dust, sand, and debris, creating a wall of dust that it hurls at anything in its path. These dust storms, which occur in all desert regions of the world, can be as big as sixty miles (97 km) wide, a mile (1.6 km) high, and can last for several hours, leaving up to a foot of sand covering everything in their wake.

More serious than dust devils—dust-filled whirlwinds—haboobs can blow at thirty miles (48 km) an hour, creating thick, choking dust clouds that cause several deaths and injuries each year, as well as millions of dollars worth of damage in North American desert regions around Arizona, Texas, and New Mexico.

it past five weeks old, but those that do survive are mature at eleven months, and the females can produce two or three litters of up to six babies each season.

THE COLORADO PLATEAU

The Colorado Plateau is a semi-arid region of southern Utah and northern Arizona, and because it is geologically distinct, experts disagree over whether it is true desert or not. One of the parts that is best known is the Painted Desert, named such because of the multitude of colors found there, from lavender to shades of gray with vibrant red, orange, and pink.

The Colorado Plateau area is a long expanse of badlands (dry terrain eroded by wind and water into canyons, gullies, and ravines) and buttes (small hills with flat tops and steep sides), large barren areas, and spectacular geological formations. Home to the Navajo and Hopi Native Americans, it covers 130,000 square miles (336,698 sq km) and is centered around the Four-Corners area, where Colorado, New Mexico, Utah, and Arizona meet.

Most of the Plateau is drained by the Colorado River,

and its most famous sites are Monument Valley and the Grand Canyon.

MONUMENT VALLEY

Monument Valley, a place the Navajo call Tse'Bii'Ndzisgaii, or Valley of the Rocks, is situated on the Arizona-Utah state line. Although it is called a valley, it is actually a wide, flat desolate landscape interrupted by huge crumbling sandstone formations rising hundreds of feet into the air. These rocky pinnacles, buttes, and mesas (flat, tablelike formations) are

Monument Valley has been the setting for more Western movies than any other site in the United States.

the remnants of the sandstone that once covered the whole area. The largest of them reaches one thousand feet (3045m) above the valley floor.

The valley, which covers over 143 square miles (370 sq km) belongs to the Navajo people and is one of the most photographed places in the world. Situated 5,564 feet (1,696 m) or more than one mile (1.6 km) above sea level, it was once a basin that was pushed up millions of years ago by underground geological activity. The sandstone surface was then eroded by wind and water, over many years, to its

present formation. The vivid red color of many rocks is due to the iron oxide in the weathered siltstone. Other rocks are colored blue-gray by manganese oxide.

GRAND CANYON: CALIFORNIA CONDORS

The Grand Canyon is a huge fissure in the Colorado Plateau carved over millions of years by the Colorado River, which winds through the bottom of the canyon. One of the natural wonders of the world, the canyon is famous for its dramatic

The Californian Condor is the rarest and
largest flying bird in North America.

size and for its beautifully preserved sequences of ancient rocks that record nearly two billion years of the geological history of North America.

The canyon is 277 miles (446 km) long, up to 18 miles (29 km) wide, and is over a mile (1,800 m) deep. Recent evidence suggests that the Colorado River established its course through the canyon at least seventeen million years ago. As the Colorado Plateau was uplifted, the river and its tributaries cut channels through layer after layer of rock.

Fed by snowmelt from the high desert plateau and the eastern slopes of the Rockies, the river carves its way through canyon country for 1,450 miles (2,334 km), crossing seven states and averaging three hundred feet (91 m) wide and one hundred feet (30 m) deep.

The canyon offers a nearly undisturbed natural habitat through a range of elevations from the river at its base, to desert to mountain forests on the rim, and it contains more than 1,500 types of plants, 350 birds, 89 mammals, 47 reptiles, 9 amphibians, and 17 species of fish.

Among the birds that make this strange desert landscape their home is the rarest and largest flying bird in North America, the California condor. They are so rare that each bird wears a tracking beacon and its own number tag. In 1987, there were only twenty-two of these magnificent birds left alive, after poaching of their eggs, lead poisoning, and perils such as power lines and habitat destruction destroyed the population. In a desperate attempt to save them, the remaining wild birds were collected for captive breeding, a program that was so successful that by May 2012, there were 405 condors, 226 of them living in the wild.

Condors have an amazing ten-foot (3 m) wingspan and they save precious energy by riding the updrafts from the great canyon walls. They are vultures that feast off the carcasses of large mammals. Ravens are often the clue that there is a deer or cow nearby that has not survived the winter. The condors will fly in, take over the carcass, and tear it apart with their giant beaks.

California condors have changed little in ten thousand years, since the time they would have been feasting from the bones of mammoths and giant sloths and scavenging from the kills of saber-toothed tigers. They nest in crevices or caves in rock faces. Females lay only one egg every two or three years, and the young birds learn to fly at about six months.

After such a close brush with extinction, it's cause for celebration that California condors once again soar across canyon country.

MOJAVE DESERT: DEATH VALLEY, COYOTE

The Mojave Desert is the transition from the cool Grand Basin Desert to the hot Sonoran, twenty-five thousand square miles (64,750 sq km) of arid desert in southeastern California, overlapping into Nevada, Arizona, and Utah.

While most of the Mojave is between three thousand and six thousand feet (914 to 1,829 m), it contains both Telescope Peak, 11,049 feet (3,368 m) high, and Death Valley, the lowest, driest, and hottest place in North America. Temperatures here have reached 134°F (56.7°C), the second highest recorded anywhere in the world, and the highest July temperatures recorded anywhere on the planet.

Although some experts do not consider the Mojave a

Coyotes are clever and adaptable
animals that can survive the sizzling
heat of Death Valley.

The Pinacate volcanic field in
Sonora has been active for two or
three million years and eruptions
have occurred as recently as
thirteen thousand years ago.

desert in its own right, it contains about two hundred plant species that are not found in the deserts to the north and south of it. Mojave yucca, desert Spanish bayonet, creosote bush, and blackbrush are common, and unlike the Sonoran Desert, there are very few trees. Despite its name the Mojave's Joshua Tree is not a tree at all but a yucca that is only found in the Mojave.

Death Valley is a long, narrow basin that lies below sea level—its deepest point is 282 feet (86 m) below—walled on either side by steep mountain ranges. In summer, it can feel like an enormous oven, with day after day of baking heat and sizzling temperatures. Its annual rainfall of 2.36 inches (60 mm) is so little, it wouldn't even fill a coffee cup.

Death Valley was given its name in 1849, after three gold rush families traveling by wagon got lost in the desert. The nights were freezing cold, and they were forced to burn their wagons. With no idea how to get out, two of the younger men set out to get help. They walked for an astonishing fifty-eight days until finally, after a grueling four-hundred-mile trek; they found an escape route over a mountain pass. They returned for their families and one survivor wrote in his journal "Goodbye Death Valley," a name that seemed so appropriate that it stuck.

In July, Death Valley is at its hottest, the average daily temperature reaches 115°F (46°C). Yet while most visitors will pass through pretty quickly, a surprising number of animals live in this most inhospitable of places.

Among them is the greatest survivor of all, the American coyote. Coyotes are clever and adaptable animals that can live in all kinds of habitats, from prairies to deserts, and forest to mountains. Halfway between the size of a fox and a wolf, they can be solitary but usually live in packs and they will eat almost anything.

Coyotes aren't popular; they have a reputation for killing livestock and pets and are sometimes seen as vermin. But in the weeks we spent filming them, our team found them to be full of character, loyal to one another, and incredibly resourceful.

In the scorching heat of Death Valley, coyotes need to be incredibly resourceful to find enough to eat, and one of the most extraordinary sights we came across was coyotes feasting on the caterpillars of the hawkmoth.

These caterpillars appear during the brief desert flowering time in April and May, and the numbers can vary hugely from one year to another. The first year we filmed,

there were so many that the roads were covered in squashed caterpillars. But in the second year, when we returned to film close-ups of coyotes eating these caterpillars, we couldn't find a single one, even though we were there at exactly the same time and the flowering was the same. This time, the coyotes were eating small, brightly colored beetles that were feeding on the flowers.

Our team was the first to document coyotes eating the caterpillars and the beetles, something that even the Death Valley National Park authorities were unaware of and a great example of just how versatile coyotes can be.

On one occasion, we spotted a coyote stalking a roadrunner—a long-legged type of cuckoo found only in North America. And in what seemed like a parody of the old *Looney Tunes* cartoons about Wile E. Coyote and the Road Runner, the roadrunner squawked and flew into a tree, while the disgruntled coyote stood under the tree, looking up as if to say, "Darn, how did I miss that one?" before slinking off.

SONORAN DESERT: HARRIS HAWKS AND CACTUS BEES

The Sonoran Desert is an arid region covering 120,000 square miles (310,799 sq km) in southwestern Arizona and southeastern California, as well as most of Baja California and the western half of the state of Sonora in Mexico. Subdivisions of this hot, dry region—the hottest of the North American deserts—include the Colorado and Yuma Deserts. Irrigation has also produced fertile agricultural areas such as the Coachella and Imperial Valleys of California. Warm winters attract tourists to the resorts of Palm Springs in California and Tucson and Phoenix in Arizona, which are also in the Sonoran.

Cacti

There are twenty-five hundred species of cacti in the world, and all but one species is found naturally only in the Americas—North, Central, South, and the Caribbean.

With their extended network of shallow roots, cacti are experts at collecting and storing the water from every drop of rain that falls. Amazingly, a square mile of desert can hide 180,000 tons of water, stored inside the cacti since the last rains. And to keep their precious water supply safe, they protect it with the most ferocious set of spines found in nature.

It is because of the great number of cacti found in the Sonoran Desert that it has a greater range of plant and animal species than any other desert in the world.

The saguaro, whose blossom is Arizona's state flower, can live up to two hundred years, grow from forty to sixty feet (12 to 18 m) tall, and can store many gallons of water because the ribs on its large stem and arms can expand. Many animals rely on the saguaro for food, feeding on the trunk, seeds, flowers, and nectar, as well as using it for shelter; Gila desert woodpeckers and gilded flickers will hollow out their nests inside it.

The saguaro, which is only found in the Sonoran Desert, is a keystone species; one that plays a critical role in maintaining the ecological community around it, and whose impact is greater than would be expected, based on its relative abundance. But contrary to popular belief, the saguaro is not the largest cactus in the world; the largest is the cardon cactus, also found in the Sonoran, and almost exclusively in the Baja California peninsula. Some of the largest cardons can grow to seventy feet (21 m) and weigh up to twenty-five tons. These very slow-growing plants can live well over three hundred years.

One of the wettest deserts in North America, the Sonoran, averages from three to sixteen inches (7.6 to 41 cm) of rain a year. It has two rainy seasons, one short and heavy in the summer, and another longer and lighter in the winter. Because of this rain, the Sonoran has more plant and animal types than any other desert in the world, including over twenty-five hundred plant species, such as the desert ironwood tree that only grows in this desert, and is a "nurse" plant to over five hundred plants and animals. A small, sparse, slow-growing tree that can live for as long as fifteen hundred years, the desert ironwood creates a microhabitat, its dense canopy lowering the temperature underneath to provide cover for desert flowers and its seeds providing food for many rodents and birds.

The Sonoran also has a wide range of cacti, and cactus spines are a real problem for Harris hawks because the small animals they prey on can hide under the spines to escape them. To outwit the prey, Harris hawks in the Sonoran have learned to hunt together in groups of two to six birds. First, the adults send the juvenile birds to flush out prey, such as rabbits, that hide under the cover of the cactus's sharp needles, and then the adult birds go in for the kill.

Just before the rains come, the cacti burst into flower. They have been storing their water reserves since the last rain, which may have been as much as eight months earlier. Now, when the desert is badly in need of water, the cactus flowers are packed with nectar, providing a vital lifeline for animals. There can be sixty gallons (227 l) of thirst-quenching nectar per acre; a gift the cactus offers in return for pollination.

The cacti flower for just one month, and this is the cue for the American cactus bee to breed. Thousands of bees gather at sites close to the cactus flowers, where up to fifty male bees fight over access to one female, forming angry balls of mating bees. Once they have mated, the females dig nesting holes in the ground. Using their heads to jackhammer through the soil, they make a hole four to ten inches (10 to 25 cm) deep, in which they carve out ten to twelve cells. In each cell, they place a lump of pollen mixed with nectar, before laying an egg and sealing the cell. When finished, they will seal the whole nest.

The job completed, the exhausted female bees will die. Just two weeks later, the young bees will hatch, the fastest journey time from egg to adult of any known bee.

The Sonoran Desert is home to one of North American's most elusive creatures. Jaguars, the third largest cats after the tiger and the lion, once roamed the United States and

Cactus spines are a
problem for Harris hawks
as the small animals they
prey on can hide under
the spines.

Some desert plants, like
the cereus, bloom at night
instead of during the day
to attract pollinators like
bats that come out at night
when the desert is cooler.

Canada, but hunting and habitat loss reduced their numbers so dramatically that for some time, it was believed there were none left north of Mexico. Then, a few years ago, it was discovered that a small group of jaguars had been traveling five hundred miles (805 km) across the desert into Arizona. One was even spotted as far north as Tucson.

Found mostly in the jungles of South and Central America, jaguars also live in the desert and travel between temporary watering holes. Beautiful and powerful, they were prominent in ancient Native American cultures in the past, when they were more common in the United States. The Olmec Indians believed the power of the jaguar's roaring could start an earthquake.

Jaguars are nocturnal and solitary and sightings are extremely unusual. To film these shy and elusive cats, we used remote camera traps. Our rare footage, obtained during ten weeks of filming over two years in a remote spot several hours from the nearest town, confirmed what several sightings over the past decade had suggested, jaguars are back in the United States.

CHIHUAHUAN DESERT: SPADEFOOT TOADS

The largest desert in North America is the Chihuahuan, most of which lies in Mexico, although in the north it extends into New Mexico, Texas, and southeast Arizona.

The Chihuahuan Desert covers an area of more than 175,000 square miles (453,248 sq km), which is bigger than the state of California, yet it is only a fifth the size of the world's biggest desert, the Sahara. No part of the Chihuahuan is less than one thousand feet (305 m) above sea level, and the vast majority lies at thirty-five hundred to five thousand feet (1,066 to 1,524 m). The Sierra Madre Occidental on the west, and the Sierra Madre Oriental on the east, block most of the moisture from the Gulf of Mexico and the Pacific Ocean.

Running through the Chihuahuan are many small mountain ranges, including the Franklins in Texas and the San Andres and Doña Anas in New Mexico. Between these mountains are valleys, and there are also river valleys, formed by the Rio Grande and the Peco Rivers, creating large fertile areas within the desert. Because of the river valleys and the contrasts in elevation, this desert has a variety of habitats that are not present in many other deserts, and a wide range of plants and animals live within its boundaries.

Like the Great Basin, this is a shrub desert; its most significant plants, found throughout the desert, are creosote bush, mesquite, agave, and ocotillo. The only plant that is endemic to the Chihuahuan Desert, meaning that it doesn't grow anywhere else, is a kind of agave called lechuguilla.

This desert has mild rains in the early winter, usually in December, and a monsoon season in the summer, with a short burst of intense rain caused by moist air that penetrates from the Gulf of Mexico. These rains are the cue for a number of desert frog and toad species to seize the day and launch into a reproductive frenzy.

Among them are the spadefoot toads. These are actually burrowing frogs that have large spade-like feet they use to dig tunnels under the sand, where they spend most of their lives in a dormant state that is similar to hibernation. They remain like this for weeks or months, and during long periods of drought, they can stay in this state for up to two years. But as soon as a rainstorm approaches, they spring into action.

The sound of thunder and the vibration of the raindrops hitting the ground are believed to be the cue that stirs the spadefoots into action. They will emerge from underground and travel toward wherever the rain has pooled—a ditch, pond, or even a large puddle. Here the males attempt to attract the

The Moving Stones of Death Valley

In the heart of Death Valley there is an astonishing phenomenon that has puzzled scientists for decades. Several huge stones, some weighing as much as 700 pounds (318 kg) regularly move, completely unaided, across the flat, dry lakebed of Racetrack Playa. These stones can travel as much as 350 yards (320 m) each year and sometimes even change direction, leaving a zig-zag trail of lines behind them. Sometimes stones don't move for two or three years, and then move several times in just a few weeks.

In the 90 years since the moving stones were discovered, many attempts have been made to see them move, so far unsuccessfully. Scientists now believe that the movement is caused by a combination of high winds and ice forming at night on the surface of the clay base, embedding the stones and shifting them as the ice melts. But the mystery of the stones has yet to be conclusively proved, and every year new attempts are made to discover what propels them and to capture their movements on film.

females with loud calls, competing with one another and with males from other species. In the drive, they scramble around, mounting any frog they can grasp. They are so desperate to reproduce that occasionally they will seize another male, or a frog from a different species. Even when the male has found a female spadefoot, other males will pile on top to create a writhing heap of frogs.

The male, clasping the female, will stimulate her to lay up to two thousand eggs, which submerge and attach themselves to vegetation in the water. The male will then deposit his sperm on them and, within as little as fifteen hours, tiny tadpoles will emerge.

To survive, the tadpole must develop into a frog before the desert sun swallows up the rainwater pools. This happens in only twelve to thirteen days, the fastest development rate of any frog or toad. The young frogs will then fill up with food and bury themselves under the sand to await the next downpour.

To film the spadefoot toads we needed to wait a couple of weeks for the rain. When it finally arrived, the water levels changed quickly and the toads emerged in such huge numbers that it was hard work not to step on them in the dark, and their calls were almost deafening.

The mating frenzy was amazing to watch—one night of wild partying before all the toads disappeared as suddenly as they had arrived.

GRAN DESIERTO, MEXICO: FRINGE-TOED LIZARDS, COSTA'S HUMMINGBIRD

The Gran Desierto in Mexico is part of the Sonoran Desert, extending across much of the northern border of the Gulf of California, covering more than twenty-two hundred square miles (5,698 sq km). It is the largest continuous wilderness area within the Sonoran Desert and is the only area in North America dominated by sand sheets and dunes with little or no vegetation.

Amazingly, this desert, with dunes that can reach as high as 393 feet (120 m), was formed from rock that came all the way from the Grand Canyon. As the Colorado River carved its way through the rock of the canyon, fragments were carried south and deposited here, creating a sea of sand that stretches as far as the eye can see.

The arrival of the monsoon
can turn a baking desert into
a torrent.

Spadefoot toads spend most of their lives dormant underground.
But when rain arrives they spring into action to search for mates.

Nectar-filled red flowers open on the ocotillo's branches, creating a red pathway across the desert for the hummingbird.

Beyond the dunes is a wilderness so bleak—seventy cubic miles (292 km) of barren lava that erupted onto the sand over a million years ago—that the *Apollo* missions of the 1960s used it as a training ground for the moon landings. One hundred extinct volcanic cinder cones scar the barren landscape of the Pinacate volcano fields, just south of the Arizona border, the hottest and driest part of the whole Sonoran Desert.

The sandy wilderness of the Gran Desierto is a hard place to call home for any creature. But the fringe-toed lizard has what it takes to survive the baking sun, fierce winds, and endless sand. It can fly over the dune crests, thanks to fringe-

over three inches (7.6 cm) long. It has two hundred miles (322 km) of desert inferno to cross to reach its breeding sites in California. And surviving this potentially deadly journey is all about timing. To manage its daunting migration, the Costa's hummingbird must rely on the ocotillo plant.

Even though it has been eight months since the last monsoon, the ocotillo has enough water reserves to come to life. Nectar-filled red flowers open on the ocotillo's branches, creating a red pathway across the desert. The ocotillo needs a pollinator and the hummingbird needs a source of energy, so they form an amazing desert partnership.

The hummingbird's tiny wings beat eighty times a second. For humans to sustain that level of activity, we would need three hundred pounds (136 kg) of food and 150 gallons (568 l) of water every day. So if this little hummingbird is to survive the desert crossing, he must visit one thousand ocotillo flowers in just one day.

And while the day is tough enough, nightfall presents an even greater challenge. As the sun sets, heat leaks from the ground. Without clouds to hold in the heat, the desert nights can be close to freezing. With their feathers fluffed to let body heat escape, the hummingbird allows its normal heart rate of five to nine hundred beats a minute to drop as low as fifty beats a minute and enters a state of torpor, dramatically slowing body functions and similar to a short-term hibernation. This way it will avoid a fuel crisis and save vital energy and water for its migration.

The returning sun heats the bird's tiny muscles and after a quick warm-up, the hummingbird is ready to continue on its epic journey across the desert.

like scales on its toes that keep it from sinking into the sand. It also has flaps over its ear openings, eyelids with interlocking scales, nostrils that can be closed and an upper jaw that overlaps the lower, all perfectly adapted to keep the sand out.

This baking wilderness is not the kind of place where you would expect to find a delicate hummingbird a little

CHAPTER SEVEN

THE FIGHT
FOR LIGHT

Long before there were grasslands, deserts, shrub lands, or tundra, the land was covered by trees. Forests have been on Earth for 385 million years. They dominated the world through much of that time, and today they still occupy 30 percent of all land area.

A healthy planet needs healthy forests. Without trees, we could not exist. They help to moderate the climate by soaking up and storing carbon dioxide while giving us oxygen. They regulate water cycles, stabilize soils and provide food, medicines, and wood. Forests also provide the habitat for many of the planet's animals and plants.

Tragically, they are being destroyed at an alarming rate; the world's forests have shrunk by 40 percent since agriculture began eleven thousand years ago, and three-quarters of this loss has been in the last two hundred years.

In North America, forest still covers two-thirds of the continent and there is a huge diversity of forest types, from the boreal forests of Canada, at the northern limit of tree growth,

to the tropical and subtropical forests of Central America, via the eastern deciduous forests and the western temperate rainforests. Even the deserts of North America have more trees than many desert areas of the world. The trees of North America have adapted to every kind of climate and habitat.

In Canada, a broad strip of boreal forest appeared after the last ice age and covers 1.5 billion acres (6 million sq km), stretching almost coast to coast and covering 278,000 square miles (720,016 sq km), representing 60 percent of Canada's land area. It is big enough to hold fourteen Californias and it accounts for a quarter of the world's remaining intact forest. This cold, northern boreal forest, also found in Russia and Scandinavia, is an immense and vitally important ecosystem that stores huge quantities of carbon and helps to regulate the world's temperature.

Further south are the deciduous forests of the eastern United States. These forests contain broadleaf trees that grow where there are four distinct seasons and lose their leaves

Tropical rainforests have been called the world's largest pharmacy, because over a quarter of natural medicines come from rainforest plants.

during the winter. Huge areas of these forests have been lost to building and agriculture; most of what remains can be found on the Appalachian Mountains and within the national parks.

On the western side of the continent, on the west-facing coastal mountains from Alaska to northern California, is the largest area of temperate rainforest on the planet. Largely coniferous, these rainforests grow where the summers are warm, the winters are cool, and there is plenty of rainfall. And it is here, on North America's West Coast, that the tallest, biggest, and oldest trees in the world are found.

The Coastal Redwoods reach astonishing heights of almost four hundred feet (122 m). A few hours away, on the slopes of the Sierra Nevada Mountains, the enormous Sequoias are almost as tall and far wider. Above them, on the Cascade Mountains, stand the ancient Bristlecone pines, the oldest recorded trees and a testament to survival.

Further south, in Central America, there are large areas of tropical rainforest. Closer to the equator than temperate rainforests, tropical rainforests are warmer and much wetter; the average rainfall can be as high as 390 inches (991 cm) a year.

Trees can live for hundreds and sometimes thousands of years, but most cannot survive without animals to disperse their seeds. In forests, a whole host of animals live within the trees' orbit and rely on their bounty. And nowhere is this more evident than in the tropical rainforests.

TROPICAL RAINFORESTS: KINKAJOUS, CAPUCHIN MONKEYS, AND MANAKIN BIRDS

Rainforests cover 6 percent of the earth's surface, yet they are home to half the animal and plant species in the world and two-thirds of all flowering plants, and they produce 40 percent of our oxygen.

Central America was once entirely covered by rainforest, and although large areas have now been cleared for agriculture and ranching, stretches of rainforest still thrive in Panama, Costa Rica, Honduras, Belize, southern Mexico, and on some islands in the Caribbean.

In the rainforest, the temperature remains in the 80s Fahrenheit (upper 20s Celsius) year-round and the rainfall is heavy. In these warm, wet conditions, there are plants and animals that are not found anywhere else.

The Central American tropical rainforest is home to more species of trees—over three hundred—than any other location in North America. The tallest trees grow to heights of two hundred feet (61 m) in order to access sunlight, while below them stand the rich and varied species of trees that make up the dense forest canopy. The majority of the trees in the canopy have smooth, thick bark because they don't need protection from water loss or from cold. Rainforest trees provide both food and shelter to a wide variety of the environment's plants and animals.

Deep in the forest, balsa trees sprout incredibly fast, growing to ten feet (3 m) or more in six months and to sixty to ninety feet (18 to 27 m) in six to ten years. Balsa trees are a "pioneer" species, one that invests all its energy in quick growth at the expense of a short life. For a long time, they were thought of as valueless, but, in fact, they are the nurses of the jungle; their broad leaves sheltering slower-growing seedlings when an area of jungle ravaged by storms is reestablishing. And, of course, the incredibly light and pliable wood that is naturally buoyant is extremely useful to us in all kinds of ways, like for making model airplanes.

Balsa lives fast and dies young, sometimes simply toppling over after only ten years. To reproduce, they enlist the help of the kinkajou, or honey bear. Balsa trees only bloom for a month or two with each large white flower opening for just one night. They are the perfect shape for the small, furry head of the kinkajou, which slurps the sugary nectar and emerges with pollen all over its face.

The kinkajou is an arboreal mammal—it lives in the trees and comes out only at night, so it can be hard to spot. Although it sleeps in family groups, it will forage alone. Weighing three

Kinkajous, aka "honey bears," are nocturnal mammals that are often mistaken for monkeys and love to eat honey and sweet nectar from flowers.

Spanish conquistadors in South America named capuchin monkeys after the "capuchin" monks back home, because they thought the animals looked like little men in brown robes with large hoods.

to ten pounds (1.3 to 4.5 kg), the kinkajou has huge, round eyes adapted for night vision and a prehensile tail that is as long as its body and as useful as a fifth hand. Climbing from branch to branch, it uses its tail to grip as well as to balance, foraging for fruit, leaves, flowers, and occasionally insects.

To film kinkajous raiding balsa flowers, we went to the rainforest of Panama. To get level with the treetops, we had to build a scaffolding tower seventy-eight feet (24 m) high, with a platform at the top. The balsa flowers come out for only two weeks of the year so, anticipating the event at the predicted time, our team climbed the ladders up to the top of the platform, set up the cameras, and waited . . . and waited. The Balsa's normal flowering time came and went and there was no sign of the flowers. The reason was that the rain was extremely heavy that year; there was so much rain that the Panama Canal was closed for the first time in twenty-one years because of the islands of debris washing through.

It was only after several weeks that the weather calmed down, the Balsa flowers opened, and the kinkajous appeared for their favorite treat.

The capuchin monkey also lives in the treetops, rarely coming down to the ground. Incredibly agile, the capuchin will forage for food in the branches, eating flowers, fruit, and occasionally birds' eggs.

Capuchin are among the most intelligent monkeys in the world, and they are sometimes kept as exotic pets and have been featured in films such as *Pirates of the Caribbean*. They are known to use rocks to crack fruit and nuts, and they sometimes use their tails like straws, dipping the tail in small pools of water in the bowls of trees and then sucking it. They also use the leaves of the piper plant to fend off mosquitoes. The leaves contain a powerful insecticide, and the capuchins will rub the leaves all over themselves.

One of their more bizarre rituals occurs at mating time. The male capuchin will rub his own urine all over himself, to signal to females that he is available.

The tropical rainforests are a haven for birds, and in Central America, there are hundreds of species. Among them is the manakin, North America's birds of paradise. There are around sixty different species of these small, beautiful birds, whose name comes from the Dutch for "small man." The males of all the species have patches of jewel-bright plumage on glossy black feathers, and they have some of the most elaborate mating displays in the animal kingdom.

We filmed the mating displays of both the red-capped manakins and the long-tailed manakins. The red-capped birds have, of course, brilliant red feathers on the tops of their heads and their dance is a mixture of moonwalking, jumps, and twirls. The long-tailed manakins are even more extraordinary. Unlike any other animal on Earth, these birds cooperate to win a female, instead of competing. After their joint acrobatic all-singing, all-dancing show, the female, if she is impressed, will choose the dominant male to mate with, and the junior male will wait for his turn, sometimes for as long as ten years, until the dominant male dies.

DECIDUOUS FORESTS: BLACK BEARS, WOOD FROGS, CHIPMUNKS, WOODPECKERS, WHITE-TAILED DEER, AND ELK

In the eastern part of Canada and of the United States on the Appalachian Mountains, the forests are deciduous. These forests are found in areas of the world that have four distinct seasons: spring, summer, autumn, and winter, and the trees adapt to cope with these environmental changes by shedding their leaves in winter and growing them in spring.

The average temperature of a deciduous forest is about 50°F (10°C) and the average amount of rainfall is thirty to sixty inches (76 to 152 cm) a year. The climate is temperate, with warm summers and cold winters.

Deciduous forests have three levels of plants. Moss, ferns, wildflowers, and other small plants can be found on the forest floor. Shrubs fill in the middle level, and hardwood trees like maple, oak, birch, elm, hickory, linden, walnut, chestnut, sweet gum, and beech make up the third level. At times, deciduous forests and coniferous forests can overlap and spruce, fir, and pine trees can be found mixed in with the hardwood trees.

Creatures of these forests include slugs and frogs, squirrels and chipmunks, raccoons and porcupines, owls, woodpeckers, deer, and black bears. The forest provides all the food they need and shelters them. Many adapt to the climate by hibernating in the winter.

In Algonquin Provincial Park, Ontario, about three hundred miles (483 k) north of Toronto, in careful cooperation with scientists, so that we wouldn't be intrusive, we shot rare footage of black bears in their winter dens. The

Porcupines

In the deciduous forests of the east, porcupines—large rodents covered with quills—climb up maple trees in spring to feed on the sugar-rich buds. They put on more weight at this time than at any other. But while the buds are nutritious, the new leaves that follow are filled with poisonous tannins. If the porcupine has eaten the leaves, the poisons disrupt its ability to metabolize salt and the result is a huge salt craving.

Every night, porcupines go on the hunt for salt. They will eat just about anything with a salty taste, including rose bushes, lily pads, garden produce, and even car tires. But their favorite salty taste is wood. They will gnaw on woodland barns or cabins, and sometimes even on garden furniture or wooden porches, so they can be regarded as pests. Over the summer months, many North American woodlands echo to "porcupine music" as their sharp incisors saw through wood to satisfy their salt craving.

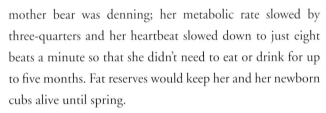

mother bear was denning; her metabolic rate slowed by three-quarters and her heartbeat slowed down to just eight beats a minute so that she didn't need to eat or drink for up to five months. Fat reserves would keep her and her newborn cubs alive until spring.

Female black bears enter their dens in October or November. Cubs are born late January and early February, weak and blind, weighing between seven ounces and one pound (198 to 454 g). They have two or three months before entering the world outside, with all its dangers, so they must grow fast.

While some animals hibernate to survive until spring, wood frogs have a unique way of dealing with the cold—they are able to freeze and thaw with their surroundings. They can lock down when surrounded by ice and go into stasis, then thaw without any damage; their blood acts like antifreeze so that instead of developing dangerous ice crystals when the temperature drops below zero, their blood remains fluid.

This is a risky strategy. If the freeze is more than a few degrees below zero, or if it lasts for too long, they will die. But their amazing ability has the cryogenics industry very excited. If frogs can do it, why not humans?

Once the thaw arrives, new life bursts out all over the forest. In Shenandoah National Park, in the Blue Ridge Mountains of Virginia, there is almost three hundred square miles (777 sq km) of deciduous forest. And when the region's black bear cubs emerge from the den for the first time in spring, a feast awaits them as the trees pump nutrients out of

Black bears are not considered to be true hibernators, because they can be easily aroused, but they do not eat, drink, defecate, or urinate while denning.

deep storage into the new buds and unfurling leaves. Foraging in the woodland, they will eat a large variety of foods. Bears are opportunists and will consume twigs, roots, berries, young plants, and buds, insects from beetles to ants to bee larvae eaten with honey, and occasionally small mammals and fish.

Most bears don't climb, but American black bears evolved in the time of megapredators, when the giant saber-tooth tigers and mammoths roamed the land. To survive, they had no choice but to climb, and they still do today. One of the cubs' first lessons will be how to scale a tree.

While the bears are learning to climb, the white-tailed deer are giving birth to their fawns.

Female deer time their breeding so that their fawns all arrive within a two-week period in May. That way, during their early days when they are exposed the most, predators will only be able to take a few. Black bears, not usually meat-eaters, will take newborn fawns because they are easy prey. In less than a week, the fawn's limbs will strengthen and they can outrun a bear. But for those first few days, they are vulnerable, so the mothers move them out of the forest and into the nearby meadows, where the bears rarely follow.

The bears may stay away, but there are plenty of other predators, chief among them the coyote, with its excellent sense of smell, so the doe has a careful strategy for keeping her fawn safe. First she will clean it, trying to remove its scent. Then she will hide it in the long grass. If a coyote appears, the doe will try to distract it from her fawn by appearing to limp, a clever deception females often use to lure predators away from their young.

At the end of the summer, as fall draws in, the chipmunks get busy. The trees are beginning one of the most dramatic transitions in nature. Before the frost arrives, each tree withdraws the green food-making chlorophyll from every leaf back into the trunk and branches. All that is left are the yellow and red leaf skeletons.

While this is happening, the oak tree produces its seed—the acorn. The average oak produces a hundred thousand acorns each year. And the chipmunk will be the oak's ally, albeit inadvertently. Chipmunks not only eat the acorns they store, but they also eat the grubs of acorn boring weevils, thereby helping the (oak's) next crop of acorns.

When our team arrived, the oak trees were literally raining acorns. Perhaps because it was an El Niño year, there was an abundance of acorns rarely seen before. They pounded on our roof all night and were a major trip hazard during the day. But the chipmunks were in heaven.

These tiny striped squirrels are only four to seven inches (10 to 18 cm) tall and weigh one to five ounces (28 to 142 g). Most would fit comfortably into a teacup. And they were in a frenzy of activity. They collect all through the fall and each one has to gather about one thousand acorns and hoard them away underground for winter. They can collect around 150 a day, and they store far more than they need.

They spin the acorns, turning them over in their paws like a baseball to make sure they're unharmed, then pop them into their cheek pouches. They can stash a surprising number of acorns in these pouches, which bulge comically as they fill up. When not another acorn can be crammed in, the chipmunk will go back to its burrow to deposit the acorns. Burrows have tiny entrances, often hidden under the roots of trees but under the ground, they can be nine to thirteen feet (3 to 4 m) long. The chipmunks keep them very clean, stashing all their debris in waste tunnels.

Every now and then, we noticed a chipmunk scanning acorns for the tell-tale hole that indicated a nice, juicy weevil

The autumn color change
across North America is the
most dramatic in the world.

Forest Fires

Boreal forests cover much of Canada's cold northern regions from the Pacific to the Atlantic. While the winters are freezing, in the hot, dry summers, these woodlands are vulnerable to giant forest fires.

The blazes can be terrifying as flames sweep through the forest at frightening speeds—up to fifty miles per hour (80 kph), and reach temperatures of more than 1,400°F (760°C). Most animals must flee or die and no tree can withstand the inferno. Every year around seven thousand square miles (18,130 sq km) is burned to ash.

But the trees capitalize on the destruction. The shape of the canopy allows the fire to pass quickly, while also stimulating the cones to release their seeds. And the cleared underbrush is the perfect place for the next generation of trees to take hold.

grub was inside. The chipmunk would open the acorn and stash the grub in its pouch until it had several. Then it sat back to eat them, savoring the joy after all its hard work. Our film footage of this was a first.

On our second visit, the following year, there were fewer acorns and battles were going on between chipmunks from rival territories. They would clash in a ball of flying fur and it would be over in seconds. They move incredibly fast, so to capture scenes like this, we filmed at nearly twenty times normal speed. When you shoot at high speed, it reveals a wealth of additional detail that isn't possible at normal speeds; in this case, we caught the chipmunks spinning in circles, stepping aside in a split second to avoid a falling acorn, and teasing and battling with one another.

Chipmunks have become a Hollywood favorite, and it's easy to see why. Their big eyes, passion for acorns, and comical behavior is endearing. And unlike many other animals, chipmunks are not hard to find, so chipmunk watching is the perfect place to start for any junior naturalist.

If chipmunks serve the oak trees well, the acorn woodpecker is its worst nightmare. This woodpecker collects its winter larder by drilling a hole in the trunk of the tree and carefully inserting an acorn into it until it is a perfect fit. As this is patiently repeated over and over again, the tree is dotted with thousands of acorns. An industrious woodpecker family of six or seven birds can create as many as fifty thousand acorn storage holes in one tree, but sadly not one will ever become another oak tree.

The end of summer often comes suddenly, and as vast cold fronts sweep down the continent and arctic air engulfs the deciduous woodland, elk herds gather

in clearings for the cows to watch their "champions" battle it out. Bulls have remained separate from the females all year until it is time to display, when bugling—making a bellowing sound similar to blowing a horn or bugle—grabs their attention. The louder and more frequently a bull bellows, the more attractive he becomes. His harem may grow to as many as twenty or more cows. If other males move in, he makes a show of physical power and bugling, and if the other doesn't back down, they will fight, antlers locked, until the weaker gives way.

Chipmunks will defend their territory and
give a shrill, birdlike chirp to warn of a threat.

Northern Flying Squirrels

One of the most successful creatures in the northern boreal forests is the flying squirrel.

Using wings of loose skin that stretch from its arms to its legs, this squirrel can glide one hundred feet (30.5 m), allowing it to move quickly and easily through the forest, even when the ground is deep in snow. This way, the squirrels can search for food when it's scarce over an area as big as twenty square miles (52 sq km), far more than a ground squirrel could manage.

There are downsides to gliding. It makes them vulnerable to attack, so they only fly at night. Because they're nocturnal, they have enormous eyes to help them see in the dark. The other downside is that these squirrels can't put on too much weight or they wouldn't be able to fly, so they don't hibernate. But this negative is outweighed by the liberation flight gives this remarkable squirrel.

It's also good news for the forest. Flying squirrels spread seeds over vast distances, helping the conifers to maintain their grip on the northern lands.

THREE EXTRAORDINARY SURVIVORS

Over on the West Coast of the United States, the forests are very different. The warmth of the ocean and the shelter of the mountains keep the ice at bay, creating constant mild, wet conditions that are perfect for tree growth. The result is the tree wonders of the world, the tallest and biggest trees on the planet. On the mountains above them, braving the elements, sit the world's oldest trees.

COASTAL REDWOOD

The coastal redwood (*Sequoia sempervirens*) forests of northern California are one of the only North American forest to have survived since the time of the dinosaurs. These forests, which stretch from the northern border of California down to Big Sur, survived the meteorite strike that wiped out so much life, including the dinosaurs, sixty-five million years ago and have thrived ever since. The conditions are tree heaven—it is never too hot, as ocean fog will damp the heat down, and never too cold, as the ocean keeps the air warm and the mountains deflect the icy northern winds. The climate is stable and there is plenty of moisture. So the redwood trees grow, and grow, and keep on growing, reaching an average of 300 to 350 feet (91 to 106 m) tall and sixteen to eighteen feet (4.8 to 5.5 m) across. The tallest redwood measured is 379.1 feet (115.5 m). These trees are not only tall, they are very old; some of them have been around for two thousand years.

If ever a forest has achieved total dominance of the earth, it is here. These trees take almost everything there is to take, and as a result, the forest is eerily quiet. The giant redwoods are so successful that they don't need animals to spread their seeds. And their vast canopy blocks out light, keeping any competition from taking root.

CALIFORNIA'S SIERRA NEVADA: GIANT SEQUOIAS

The giant sequoia tree (*Sequoiadendron giganteum*) is also a redwood, a close cousin of the coastal redwood. Growing on the lower slopes of the Sierra Nevada Mountains in California, these are the largest trees on the planet in terms of total volume. They grow to heights of up to 311 feet (95 m) and an astonishing fifty-six feet (17 m) in diameter, giving them a greater girth than any other tree and a greater volume of wood.

Growing at an altitude of over three thousand feet (914 m) above sea level, there is no sea fog to cushion the lives of these trees, and deep snow can carpet them in winter. But their giant size and longevity has allowed them to dominate.

The oldest known sequoia has been standing for thirty-five hundred years. Like the coastal redwood, the sequoia is a conifer that produces as many as eleven thousand cones on a single tree. But unlike the redwoods, they need an ally for their continuing survival, and it comes in the unlikely guise of fire. Sequoia seedlings can only grow in full sunlight with no competition from other plants. Forest fires not only open the seeds for dispersal, they also ignite the dry land

Redwood forests are the best of all forests at capturing carbon dioxide from the atmosphere and locking away the carbon in their wood.

in the dead of summer and the sequoias, while singed, are unharmed, their fire-resistant bark keeping them safe while the blaze destroys any competitors, leaving the space clear for new sequoias to seed.

BRISTLECONE PINES

The third great survivor, the bristlecone pine, is also a conifer. This tree's claim to fame is not size but age; the oldest has been standing for almost five thousand years, longer than the oldest of the Egyptian pyramids.

Bristlecone pines—the name refers to the dark purple cones that have prickles on their surface—predominantly grow high up on the Cascade Mountains that shelter the coastal redwoods. Where they stand, it is a long way from tree heaven, and more like tree hell. At over six thousand feet (1,829 m) and sometimes as high as nine thousand feet (2,743 m), growing in small groves, the bristlecone pines endure the full force of North America's climatic fury.

Their survival strategy is simply endurance. Gnarled, twisted, and stunted, they are surprisingly strong; their wood is very dense and resinous, and is resistant to invasion by insects, fungi, and other potential pests. Rather than grow large, they put their resources into surviving, growing only a hundredth of an inch a year.

COASTAL TEMPERATE FORESTS: COASTAL WOLVES

The North American temperate rainforest grows on west-facing coastal mountains from Kodiak Island in Alaska to northern California, and is the largest temperate rainforest in the world.

There are only a few such forests and their ecosystem is so productive that the biomass—the biological material that includes trees, mosses, shrubs, and soils—can be four times greater than that of any comparable area in the tropics.

In British Columbia, Canada, the giant Sitka spruce grows along the banks of rivers in the Great Bear Rainforest. These trees can grow three times faster than average because of one special nutrient, that reaches them in the most unusual way.

Every fall, vast shoals of salmon journey up these rivers to spawn. And the wolves that live in the forest come down to the rivers to practice their fishing skills. Wolves don't usually catch and eat fish. But these wolves, which are slightly smaller with proportionately bigger feet, are a race

A giant sequoia tree named General Sherman is the largest living being on Earth. It is 275 feet (84 m) tall and has a circumference of 101.7 feet (31 m) at the base and a volume of nearly 52,972 cubic feet (481 m3).

apart, honed for life in the Pacific rainforest.

Once they've caught the fish, the wolves will often carry it into the forest before eating the energy-rich brain, leaving the rest to break down, flood the soil with nutrients and feeding the giant trees.

To record footage of the wolves catching salmon required patience and careful planning. This was our most challenging shoot of all the forest sequences, and took nine or ten weeks, over two years. With the support of a scientific expert and two experienced First Nation guides, both of whom knew the land and the animals, our team, assistant producer Mandi Stark and cameramen Rolf Steinmann and Shane Moore, had first to find the wolves in the vast and remote stretch of river and forest, and then had to stay downwind of them while waiting for low tide, when the wolves would fish. If the wolves saw or caught wind of us, they would vanish. If the tide was out or the wind changed direction, we could only wait.

Coastal wolves
in Canada's Great Bear
Rainforest are the
only ones that will catch
and eat salmon.

To be in the right place at the right time required both luck and judgment. Although there were key spots the wolves would use, a number of factors would affect where they would fish on any given day, including the tide, the weather, and the number of salmon.

This rainforest, the largest intact coastal temperate rainforest on the planet, is astonishingly beautiful, but it's not called rainforest for nothing—it rained nonstop. The rain, while making life pretty uncomfortable, did have some advantages, such as helping to mask our sound and smell as we tracked the wolves.

Both our cameramen had filmed wolves before, and both of them would mimic the wolves' howl to draw them out—a skill that takes time to perfect. Rolf in particular was exceptional at this, and his howl proved very effective in attracting wolves to the water's edge.

BOREAL FORESTS: POLAR BEARS

The Canadian boreal forest system, the largest forest area in North America, stretches right across the country from coast to coast. There is more intact forest in the Canadian boreal than in the Brazilian Amazon, and the forest is the largest area of wetlands in any ecosystem in the world; it contains more lakes and rivers than any similar-sized landmass on Earth.

The coniferous trees of the boreal forest are built for total extremes. Their conical shape reduces snow buildup, which might break their branches, and their needles have thick waxy coatings and a small surface area, to resist cold winds and minimize water loss, an important consideration in places where, although there is a lot of water, it may be frozen for much of the year.

These conifers include fir, pine, spruce, hemlock, aspen, birch, and larch. All of these tree types bear cones that carry their seeds. When the cones open either by falling, or because a bird or mammal opens them, the seeds are dispersed.

In the northern reaches of the boreal forests, the bitterly harsh winters stunt the growth of the trees. These are the last forests before the northern extremes where trees can no longer grow. They include the only woodlands in the world that shelter polar bears, and represent the southern limit of where they are able to live.

Hudson Bay ices over every winter for up to eight months. The polar bears live on the ice, but as the pack ice retreats north in June, they come ashore, around the town of Churchill in Manitoba, and wait for four or five months, living in semihibernation, until the bay ices over again. As they congregate on the shores, ready to return to the ice, it is the largest gathering of polar bears—usually solitary animals—anywhere in the world.

Pregnant females that come ashore make their dens in the forest, where they have their young. They don't return to the ice in the fall with the rest of the polar bears; they stay in the forest dens in semihibernation, nursing their cubs for another four months, until around March, when the cubs weigh around twenty-two to thirty-three pounds (10 to 15 k) and are strong enough to follow their mothers back onto the sea ice in the bay, for the spring seal-hunting season.

This is the largest polar bear denning site in North America, and one of the three largest denning sites in the world. Hundreds of female polar bears den here. Unlike

Polar bear fur is white, but their skin is black which helps it absorb heat from the sun. They have huge, webbed feet that act as oars when swimming, and as snowshoes when walking across thin ice.

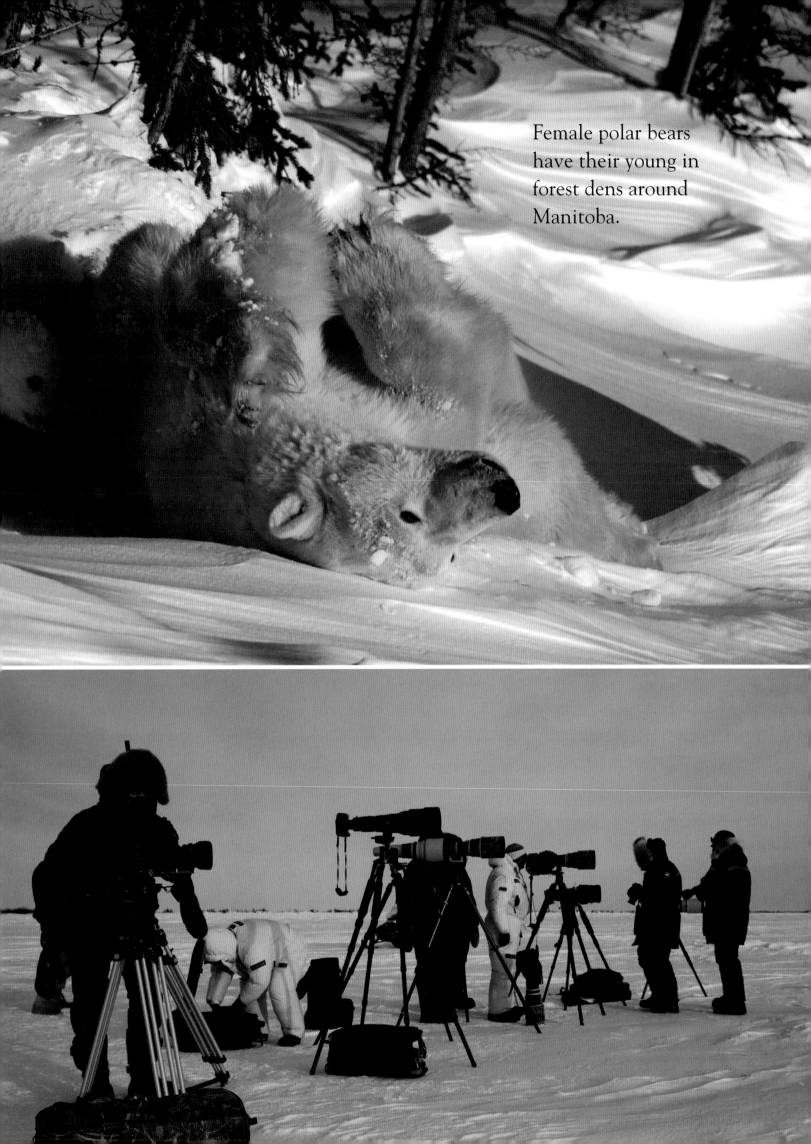

Female polar bears have their young in forest dens around Manitoba.

bears further north that use snow drifts as birthing sites, the bears here dig hollows in the peat along the banks of lakes and streams, under the shelter of the spruce trees. The tree roots hold the roof of the den together and prevent it from collapsing.

Polar bears have been coming to Hudson Bay for thousands of years, and people travel from all over the world to see them as they make their way back out to the ice. This population of bears is one of thirteen subpopulations, or communities of polar bears in North America, which together represent 70 percent of all the world's polar bears.

There are an estimated twenty thousand polar bears in the world. The most carnivorous member of the bear family, they spend most of their time at the edges of pack ice where seals are abundant and accessible.

NORTH AMERICA

From the tiny, mouse-like pika to the sleek grey bottle-nosed dolphin, from the coiled rattlesnake to the spotted jaguar—all thrive within North America's mosaic of ecosystems. It is a place as famed for its vastness as for its grains of sand, mythicized for both its snow-capped Rockies and carpeted snowy tundras. Though only the third-largest continent, North America boasts more of the Seven Natural Wonders of the World than any other, three in total: the Aurora Borealis, which phosphorescently paints the northern skies of Greenland and Canada; the Grand Canyon, with its sweeping Arizona depths and unforgettable sunset hues; and Paricutin, Mexico's active cinder cone volcano.

The landmass' greatest wonder, though, is its immense diversity. It is home to deserts and forests, mountains and plains, lakes, rivers, and oceans. We, a team of dedicated natural history filmmakers and cameramen, traversed them all in hopes of encountering just some of its hundreds of thousands

of species. It took us three work-filled years, but we did just that. We have shown the crisp beauty of an arctic wolf in mid-stride and the dusty charge of a herd of American bison, the curious serenity of a prairie dog sniffing at a flower, and the mesmerizing queerness of a jumping spider's myriad eyes. We have shown glacial North America and North America caught in the gales of a tropical hurricane, North America in the foaming crash of sea waves and North America ignited with the reds of a blazing wildfire. And we have shown our own human markings in the midst of it all: the smallness of our footprints next to the pug marks of an arctic polar bear, dozens of mayflies adding texture to the back of our crewmember's shirt, our white 4x4 sinking into muddy jungle depths.

In snow, rain, and shine, North America is a continent unlike any other. May there always be something new to discover.

ACKNOWLEDGMENTS

Thanks to Silverback Films and the production teams behind the North America programs:

Keith Scholey, Executive Producer
Huw Cordey, Series Producer
Jane Hamlin, Head of Production
Jenni Collie, Production Manager
Adam Chapman, Producer (Plains & Rivers)
Justin Anderson, Producer (Deserts & Mountains)
Mark Brownlow, Producer (Coasts)
Emily Winks, Production Coordinator
  (Forests, Deserts, Coasts)
Rebecca Coombs, Production Coordinator
  (Mountains, Plains, Opening)
Stacey Hill, Production Coordinator (Rivers)
Alicia Decina, Assistant Producer (Deserts, Rivers)
Ed Charles, Assistant Producer (Plains, Mountains)

Jonathan Smith, Assistant Producer (Coasts, Deserts)
Nick Lyon, Assistant Producer (Plains, Opening)
Ben Wallis, Assistant Producer (Opening, Forests)
David Heath, Researcher (Coasts, Mountains)
Mandi Stark, Assistant Producer (Forests) and
  Researcher (Rivers)
Jim W. Tharp, Kit Coordinator
Dan Clamp, Technical Manager
Owen Porter, Edit Assistant
Helen Healy, Production Manager
Becky Wallis, Production Coordinator
Elly Salisbury, Production Coordinator
Cate Donnegould, Production Team Assistant
Evie Wright, Researcher
Joe Stevens, Producer (Coasts)

For Discovery Channel:

Eileen O'Neill, President
Christine Weber, Vice President, Executive Producer
Iain Riddick, Series Producer
Sarah Hume, Vice President, Production Management
Paul Gasek, Executive Producer
Max Salomon, Producer, Writer
Sarah Kass, Producer, Writer
Kris Kral, Producer, Editor
Kristin Wilcox, Associate Producer

For Animal Planet:

Marjorie Kaplan, President and General Manager
Jason Carey, Vice President, Production
Mick Kaczorowski, Executive Producer
Jamie Linn, Associate Producer

Our thanks to the very skilled cameramen and women who worked with us to create the images:

Alastair MacEwen
Alonso Sánchez
Andy Shillabeer
Barrie Britton
Chris Chanda
David Reichert
Dawson Dunning
Didier Noirot
Doug Anderson
Gavin Thurston
Henry Mix
Ivo Nörenberg

Jamie McPherson
Jeff Hogan
Jeff Turner
John Aitchison
John Shier
Justin Maguire
Kevin Flay
Mark Payne-Gill
Mark Smith
Mark Yates
Martyn Colbeck
Matt Aeberhard

Michael Kelem
Neil Rettig
Nick Guy
Oliver Goetzl
Paul Atkins
Paul Stewart
Richard Burton
Richard Wollocombe
Rod Clarke
Rolf Steinmann
Ron Chappel
Scott Snider

Shane Moore
Simon Werry
Sinclair Stammers
Sophie Darlington
Stephen De Vere
Sterling Johnson
Steve Kroschel
Ted Giffords
Warwick Sloss
Tim Shepherd

We would like to extend enormous thanks to the many experts we worked with who have spent a lifetime studying specific weather patterns or individual animal behavior and who were extremely generous in sharing this knowledge with us and acting as our guides and advisers.

Finally thanks to Caro Handley for her help in putting together the *North America* series book. And thanks to the Running Press team: Publisher Christopher Navratil, Editor Geoffrey Stone, Associate Publisher and Marketing Director Craig Herman, Publicist Seta Zink, and Designer Melissa Gerber.